Island of One

Island of One

Born Different. Built to Thrive.

JASON MCCLAIN

Breakthrough
—PUBLISHING—

Copyright ©2025 Jason McClain
All rights reserved.

Island of One
Born Different. Built to Thrive.

ISBN: 979-8-9993163-4-9 *Paperback*

Published by
BREAKTHROUGH PUBLISHING, INC.
www.breakthroughpublishing.net

Printed in the United States of America.
All rights reserved under International copyright Law.

Contents and/or cover may not be reproduced in whole or in part in any form without the express written consent of the Author.

DEDICATION

I dedicate this book to —

Jesus Christ and every person I have met who has become a part of the fabric of my life.

My wife, **Sofia**, who stood by me and loved me when everyone else ran.

My children, **Kayla, Savanna,** and **Mackenzie** who always had a word of encouragement for me.

My friends, **Bill, Ron, Dave, Von, Mark,** and **Jeff** who supported me every day and at every turn.

My mother, **Sylvia**, who showed me what love and family really means. Without her, I would never have become the individual I am today.

My father, **Joseph**, who took the time to introduce me to philosophers that helped me put words to my path.

My three brothers, **Joe, John, Mike,** and sister, **Gayle**, whom, as a kid growing up, were the ones I watched.

INTRODUCTION: The Call to Your Island

CONTENTS

INTRODUCTION
The Call to Your Island 13

PART I
Discovering Your Sovereign Territory

CHAPTER I
Discovering Your Sovereign Territory 29
CHAPTER II
Seizing the Helm of Your life 38

PART II
The 7 Keys to Thriving on Your Island

CHAPTER III
C is for Clarity (Your Plan)
Charting A Deliberate Course 50
    Step-by-Step Guide to Your Personalized "Thrive Plan" 57
CHAPTER IV
O is for Ownership (Your Gifts)
Unearthing Your Innate Gifts 64

Working out with weights ... 69
Trying to Surf or Swim ... 70
Playing Golf ... 73
Riding a Motorcycle ... 75
Flying an Airplane ... 77
Playing a Guitar ... 79

CHAPTER V
M is for Manage (Your Time)
Mastering Your Time ... 90
    Practical Ways to Live with Intention: Setting Goals & Focusing ... 96
    Eliminating the "Noise" to Hear Your Own Inner Guidance ... 98

CHAPTER VI
P is for Perspective (Your Past)
Transforming Anchors into Launchpads ... 101
    Techniques for Reframing Memories into Lessons of Strength ... 111
    Understanding How Your Past Influences Your "Island" ... 112
    "Take Back the Power in Your Pain and Use It to Pave the Way." ... 113

CHAPTER VII
A is for Acknowledge (Your Fears)
Befriending the Storms & Fears ... 117
    Simple Techniques for Handling Anxiety and Fear ... 123
    Building Your Courage Muscle, One Step at a Time ... 127

CHAPTER VIII
S is for Satisy (Your Needs)
Honoring Your Core Needs ... 132
    A Little Self-Check-in: What Do You Need Most Right Now? ... 140
    Simple Ways to Nurture Your Needs on Your "Island of One" ... 142

CHAPTER IX
S is for Strengthen (Your Beliefs)
Reshaping Your Needs ... 147
    1. Identify the Belief: Become a Detective of Your Own Mind ... 157
    2. Let's Challenge the Belief: Cross-Examine with Compassion ... 158
    3. Let's Transform the Belief: You're the Author Now! ... 159

INTRODUCTION: The Call to Your Island

PART III
Action, Insight, and Transformation

CHAPTER X
Your COMPASS in Practice: The Scoring System and Validating Your Choices..168

CHAPTER XI
Action, Insight, and Transformation...195
    Creating a "Daily Thrive Ritual"..205
    Overcoming Inertia and the Gentle Resistance to Change............ 207
    The 5-Second Rule and Other "Get Started" Techniques................209

CHAPTER XII
How to Bounce Forward, Not Just Back..212
    The Resilience Engine: Bounce Forward, Not Just Back 212
    Feedback, Not Indictment—Learning from Life's Detours 213
    Embracing Challenges as Stepping Stones..215
    Setbacks as Setups for Greater Triumphs 217
    Actionable Strategies..219
    Building Your Support System (Connection is Key):......................... 222
    NFL Player's Wisdom: "You Must Have Short-Term Memory": 223

CHAPTER XIII
You are Built to Thrive..228
    Fully Owning Your Magnificent Design!..228
    The Core Message: "God Already Gave What You Need" 229
    Your Uniqueness: Your Island as a Testament to Your Design 231
    The Shift from External Validation to Internal Knowing....................234
    Actionable Strategies: Owning Your Design......................................236
    Practices for Cultivating Self-Compassion and Self-Acceptance: .237
    Journaling Prompts to Acknowledge Your Progress Strengths:....238

Creating a "Thrive Manifesto" for Your Life: 240
Example of a "Thrive Manifesto" snippet: 241

PART IV
Beyond Your Island - Connecting, Contributing, and Conuing The Journey

CHAPTER XIIV
Your Island as a Beacon 246
    Shining Your Light for Others 246
    Authentic Connection from a Place of Wholeness, Not Lack 247
    How Your Story Can Inspire and Support Others 251
    Fulfillment from Using Your Gifts to Make an Impact 256
    A Guiding Example of Purpose in Action 259

CHAPTER XV
Living a Life of Purpose and Meaning, Every Single Day 262
    Integrating the 7 Keys into the Fabric of Your Daily Life 263
    Strategies for Long-Term Growth and Preventing Backsliding 269
    Embracing Lifelong Learning and Adaptation as Your Adventure ...273
    Final Call to Action: "Are you ready to make it count?" 275

CHAPTER XVI
Lead Your Life: Speaking, Coaching, & Mentorship 278

CONCLUSION
Your Thriving Life Awaits 282
JOIN THE ISLAND 286
LISTEN TO THE CRUSH & CLIMB PODCAST 290
ABOUT THE AUTHOR 295

INTRODUCTION: The Call to Your Island

INTRODUCTION
The Call to Your Island

The Challenge of Choices and the Blueprint for Your Life

Ever found yourself replaying moments in your mind, thinking, "Man, I wish I'd done that differently!" It's a super common, nagging feeling, isn't it? Got some regrets about past decisions? What if you really had a time machine, like the fantastical one H.G. Wells dreamed up in his classic novel, The Time Machine? Imagine hitting that button, going back in time, and getting a do-over with all the wisdom you've collected since then. If you could actually zip back, knowing what you know now about life, about people, about consequences—oh man, what choices would you totally tweak? Maybe it's that career path you hesitated on, or that big opportunity you let slip by. Perhaps it's a conversation you wish you'd handled differently with a loved one, or even those small, daily habits you let slide that added up over time. It's wild to think about, isn't it? The sheer power of hindsight is just mind-blowing.

No real time machine, unfortunately! And that's a tough pill to swallow, isn't it? We can't rewind the clock to fix that awkward moment, unsay that hasty word, or grab that missed opportunity. Life doesn't come with a 'redo' button, which means every choice, every path we walk down, is the path. It really puts the pressure on, doesn't it? We've all been there, wishing we could just hit 'undo' on a particular decision, but that's just not how it works. Our past is set, and the future is built, piece by piece, by the decisions we make right now. As the philosopher Søren Kierkegaard wisely put it, "Life can only be understood backwards; but it must be lived forwards."

You know, it's like we're constantly sifting through the echo of old mistakes. Did that shaky business venture a decade ago make us shy away from a great opportunity last year? Or maybe that biting comment from a family member long ago still dictates how we react in certain social situations? It's fascinating—and sometimes frustrating—how our past, especially those moments we consider "wrong," can subtly (or not so subtly) pull the strings on our present actions. And then there's the whole "what will they think?" game. How often do we let what our parents, friends, colleagues, or even random social media influencers might say or do, sneak into our decision-making process? We want to be accepted, to belong, and sometimes that desire for external validation can unintentionally steer us away from our true north. But deep down, there's also this undeniable urge, isn't there? This yearning to really step into our own skin, to radiate confidence, to be that "peacock in the room"—not for arrogance, but because we finally own who we are and what we stand for. It's about being truly authentic, making choices that scream "this is me!" rather than "this is what they want me to be." It's about shaking off the chains of past errors and external pressures, and instead, choosing a path that feels inherently, reliably, right for you.

Often, we feel like we're constantly trying to fit into a mold,

INTRODUCTION: The Call to Your Island

chasing after those seemingly perfect ideals—the flawless career, the picturesque family, the life free of struggle—that always seem just out of reach, like shimmering mirages? In this pursuit of what's 'normal,' many of us end up feeling quite isolated, grappling with unique challenges that make us feel different or 'less than.' I call these our personal 'islands.' They're often invisible to others; people might see a smile or a confident stride, but deep down, these islands of personal struggle, doubt, or unique circumstances are very real to us. It's easy to feel marooned, watching the mainland where everyone else seems to glide through life with effortless grace.

My personal island, however, decided to announce itself with a bit more visibility. I was born without fingers on my left hand. And I quickly learned that the world is overwhelmingly designed for two hands. Simple things others took for granted—like tying shoelaces, buttoning a shirt, or catching a ball—became daily hurdles, constant reminders of my difference. Every new place, every new group of people, brought with it those quiet *(or sometimes not-so-quiet)* stares and questions. I didn't choose this path; it was just the undeniable reality I had to face every single day.

But here's the crucial point: my entire life has been about finding a way to get things done because I was born with one hand. This made me an expert in resilience and navigating any obstacle. And that brings me to the 'Island of One' idea. This concept crystallized for me one evening after watching the powerful documentary "Deaf President Now." I was profoundly moved by the story of the student protests at Gallaudet University that led to the appointment of the first deaf president and ultimately became a catalyst for the Americans with Disabilities Act. It was an incredible demonstration of collective strength, of a community coming together to demand change. Witnessing their unified voice, their shared experience of a world not designed for them, and their triumphant collective action was deeply inspiring. Yet, as I watched, a stark and personal realization hit me: I didn't have a group. There was no collective "us" for people born with one hand, no established community or shared cultural identity to lean on, no ready-made solutions passed down through generations. I wasn't like anyone else in a way that offered immediate kinship or a pre-defined path forward. I had never met anyone with one hand who had to identify the specific, intricate obstacles presented by daily life and then, without a blueprint, find a path around or through them entirely on their own. In that moment of profound contrast, I truly understood that my journey was uniquely my own—an "Island of One."

This "Island of One" isn't just about physical differences; it's a universal truth about individual responsibility in a world of constant choices. Whether you're an entrepreneur navigating the unpredictable currents of the market, a dedicated spouse making daily decisions that shape your partnership, a parent guiding your children through life's complexities, or simply an individual trying to forge a meaningful path, you are making countless choices every single day. These aren't just grand, life-altering decisions; they are the myriad small, often unconscious choices that accumulate, shaping your reality. Success in business, harmony in family life, and fulfillment in relationships all hinge on the reliability of these daily choices.

It's more than just feeling isolated. It's a profound, sometimes surprising, and ultimately empowering realization that, at your core, you are responsible for all of your choices and all of your opportunities. We can't control everything life throws at us, but we absolutely own how we react, how we see things, and where

INTRODUCTION: The Call to Your Island

we go next. That first jolt of realizing this—the weight of being fully accountable—can feel heavy. But as you truly let it sink in, that weight transforms into amazing freedom! It means you're not just passively sitting back in your own life story, tossed around by fate. Instead, the decision to do anything significant rests entirely and squarely with you. Every thought you purposely choose to think, every action you take (or bravely don't take!), every little way you interpret life's events—it all stems from your own power to act. Deep down, you are truly an island of one, the sole captain of your ship, steering through calm waters and wild storms, and the only architect of your inner world. This profound understanding means that the power to change, to grow, to truly thrive, doesn't depend on outside approval or permission; it's already, and always has been, right there inside you.

I still vividly recall a specific incident during a second-grade kickball game. A kid, in the unfiltered cruelty often found in youth, called me a "one-handed-monkey." That moment, etched in my memory, was excruciatingly painful. It was a direct hit, aimed at my most vulnerable point. I could have retreated into myself, accepting this label as my truth. But something shifted within me. My mother's words, spoken many times before, echoed with newfound power: "You're more than what you were born as." These weren't just comforting platitudes; they were a fierce declaration of my inherent worth and boundless potential. She armed me with the profound understanding that my physical difference did not define my capabilities or my identity.

That day, instead of succumbing to pain and humiliation, I channeled my fury—not in violence, but with a white-hot determination to prove that kid, and anyone else who thought like him, utterly wrong. That day marked a pivotal turning point. It was the day I made a choice: I would meet every challenge head-on, defy expectations, and redefine what was possible for me. It was the day I decided I would not be a victim of my circumstances but the master of my own destiny, refusing to let the limitations imposed by others—or by my own fears—dictate the trajectory of my life. This reality of being an "Island of One" by birth, I came to understand, meant I was designed to overcome everything. Every moment, every opportunity, every perceived obstacle, became a puzzle I had to solve.

My experience with one hand—being forced to figure out how to play guitar, devising unique fingerings and strumming techniques; learning to pilot an airplane, adapting controls and procedures; or even mastering the everyday act of cutting my food with precision—became the unconventional lens through which I stumbled upon a fundamental and profoundly liberating truth: we are all, in fact, "born with everything you need to live a life of purpose and meaning." These weren't just tasks I accomplished; they were profound lessons in adaptation, innovation, and the sheer power of will. Your perceived limitations, your personal "island," is not a prison built to confine your spirit. It is not a declaration of defeat before you even begin. If your island feels like a prison, it's only because you've allowed the external world, or your own internal doubts, to convince you of its bars. In reality, it is not a barrier to success but can be the very crucible—the intense, transformative forge—that shapes and tempers unstoppable resilience. The perceived disadvantage, the very thing that makes you feel separate or less equipped, can, through conscious effort and a shift in perspective, become your most formidable strength. Just as I had to invent my own methods, to disregard conventional wisdom and carve out my own solutions, you too have to figure out a path, absolutely unique to your life, your circumstances, and your specific challenges, on how to succeed.

INTRODUCTION: The Call to Your Island

This constant need to "figure it out" isn't unique to me, but for me, it's a daily, tangible reality. After spending a lifetime making choices on how to navigate a two-handed world, and every day trying to find a way through another unique choice, I realized I needed more than just improvisation; I needed a system. I needed a reliable system, a concrete plan I could truly depend on, to help me navigate the ceaseless stream of choices I need to make and to ultimately create a life without regret. This is precisely what the seven keys are designed to provide. Take my birthday in 2025, for instance. After a wonderful evening with my family, the one thing I was truly looking forward to was a nice, big, juicy steak. So, I seasoned the steak and was ready to take it out to the grill. But before I even stepped outside, I had to pause and plan: How was I going to carry the steak? What would I do with the spatula? I made sure I was wearing pants with pockets so I could tuck the spatula away. Only then could I confidently head out to the grill and begin. This simple act highlights a profound truth: everything we do, everything we see, often presents its own set of challenges. And we all, whether born with one hand or two, must constantly find a path to navigate those challenges. For some, it might be the immediate logistics of grilling; for others, it's thinking through the next few steps of their life if they make a decision today.

My father served 49 years in the Army and the U.S. government, which meant our family traveled all over the world. Before I even got out of high school, I had been to 27 different countries and attended 13 different schools, including in Berlin, Germany, before the Wall came down. Every single school was a chance to start over, and honestly, it wasn't always fun. Being born differently, without fingers on one hand, I was often a subject for ridicule. But the one undeniable lesson I learned by traveling from country to country, town to town, is that every day, you have a chance to hit the reset button. You truly come to realize that you are an island of one. It's all up to you. You can decide to be happier or to reset, to grow, or to fall.

This need to find a path, to overcome, is a universal human experience. One evening, my wife and I settled down to watch a movie. She wanted something unique, something she'd never seen, so I put on Rudy. My wife, not having grown up in America, had never encountered this story of the ultimate underdog, a young man who refused to quit and never gave up on his improbable dream. As the film unfolded, tears streamed down her face. In that moment, it became powerfully clear: everyone, in their own way, is an underdog. Everyone has a dream. Everyone is striving to carve out a path to find happiness and fulfillment. Regardless of our starting point, our personal "island" is where we discover our resilience, our capacity for adaptation, and the unwavering belief in our own unique journey.

Get Ready to Meet The COMPASS System!

This realization about personal islands and finding your own path became even more profound when I observed my amazing oldest daughter, Kayla. Oh, how I love that girl. Kayla is a truly gifted designer, she has an absolutely amazing fashion sense, and she's just incredible with people. What truly stands out is her uncanny ability to engage anyone on both an emotional and an intellectual level. But, my heart would ache a little when I saw her struggle. When it came to her design work in college, or even just trying to map out a path for herself, she would tirelessly seek an opinion from every single person. She just didn't have the confidence in her own brilliant decisions.

This struggle made me, as her dad, really ask: Why is making decisions so incredibly difficult for us? Why do truly talented people, like my Kayla, sometimes get stuck in first gear, unable to move forward in life? And why does it seem there's no real solution for helping people make choices that are genuinely best for them, beyond what they read online, see on TV, or absorb from TikTok and Instagram? It feels like the whole world is influencing our children, our friends, and everyone around us, pulling them in a million directions. To help my sweet Kayla, and truly, to help all the beautiful souls out there like her, I wanted to create a plan, a program, something that would help her make decisions faster and quicker. I wanted her to truly realize that she has all the tools she needs, right within her. So, this **C.O.M.P.A.S.S. System** was built not just for you, but from the deepest part of my heart, for my daughter and for every single person out there who is struggling to figure out what path they should go down, to help them realize they were born with everything they need, and to lovingly, uncandidly, open that door to understand it.

I believe it's time to take back that power. It's time to make choices that truly work for us, to make a decision to build a better life on our own terms.

This book is born from that understanding. It is not solely my personal story of navigating a unique physical challenge, though that journey forms its heart. More importantly, it's a universal blueprint, a guide for anyone who has ever felt fundamentally different, overlooked, stuck, or paralyzed by circumstances, past failures, or the suffocating weight of internal doubts. Have you ever felt trapped in a cycle, knowing you should act but not knowing how to break free? Or perhaps allowed your past to pave the way for the choices you make today? Maybe, sometimes, it just feels easier to exist than to truly thrive.

What if I told you that everything in your life, right now, can change today, simply if you allow yourself to do what is natural—to tap into the inherent power of choice you already possess? This book will serve as your comprehensive blueprint and provide you with the tangible, actionable tools necessary to navigate your own unique island, overcome any challenge, no matter how daunting it appears, and ultimately, to turn your entire life around.

Get ready to meet **The C.O.M.P.A.S.S. System!** This is the cool, actionable framework we'll use to systematically explore seven fundamental keys that are just waiting to unlock your potential. These aren't some abstract, "woo-woo" concepts; they're seriously practical levers for real, tangible change in your daily life. Let's break down how each piece of **C.O.M.P.A.S.S.** works its magic:

C is for Clarity (Your Plan): This key is all about getting super clear on your vision, setting those goals that truly light you up, and actually charting a deliberate course for where you're headed. No more just drifting along; we're talking about a roadmap you can actually follow!

O is for Ownership (Your Gifts): Here, we'll dive deep into unearthing your innate gifts, talents, and unique qualities. It's about owning who you are, recognizing the strengths forged by your past, and truly understanding that you've got everything you need inside you to rock your world.

M is for Manage (Your Time): Time flies, right? This key helps you master your time, manage distractions like a pro, and make sure you're spending your precious minutes on stuff that genuinely matters. It's about being productive and purposeful, not just busy.

P is for Perspective (Your Past): We all have a past, but it doesn't have to be a chain holding you back. This key helps you transform

INTRODUCTION: The Call to Your Island

those old anchors into powerful launchpads by shifting your perspective. You'll learn to see past experiences as valuable lessons, not burdens, and use them to propel you forward.

A is for Acknowledge (Your Fears): Let's be real, fears pop up for everyone. This key is about befriending those storms and fears, truly acknowledging them, instead of letting them paralyze you. It's about cultivating courage and building resilience so you can stride forward even when things feel a little shaky.

S is for Satisfy (Your Needs): Understanding and honoring your core needs is a game-changer. This key guides you in consciously meeting those fundamental human needs—for security, connection, growth, and more—so you can feel genuinely satisfied and well-balanced, leading to choices that truly nourish your soul.

S is for Strengthen (Your Beliefs): Last but not least, this key is all about reshaping your beliefs. You'll learn to identify those sneaky limiting beliefs that might be holding you back and actively strengthen empowering ones. Because when you truly believe in your potential, anything is possible!

If you understand what each of these COMPASS keys truly means, and, crucially, how to work with it actively and intentionally, there will be nothing you cannot accomplish, create, or fundamentally change in your life. This book isn't just a read; it's a practical guide to making those critical choices and truly understanding them. Think of it less like a personality test that just reveals who you are (though self-awareness is cool!), and more like a super dynamic decision test. It's designed to ensure that with every step, every choice, you're building a future that perfectly aligns with your deepest purpose and all those amazing things you desire. And in the pages that follow, you'll learn the precise scoring method to quantify this alignment, a revolutionary way to make your internal wisdom tangible and actionable. These keys are where we begin, to equip you with the fundamental tools you need to thrive forward.

Within these pages, you'll find not just fleeting inspiration, but a treasure trove of tangible, actionable strategies—practical exercises, mental frameworks, and step-by-step guides designed to move you from understanding to application. We'll explore, in depth, how to meticulously identify and courageously transform those limiting beliefs that have, perhaps unconsciously, acted as invisible fences around your potential. Furthermore, we will delve into the process of how to take back the power from your pain— whether it stems from past failures, betrayals, or deep-seated insecurities—and transmute that raw energy into fuel for your journey forward.

Remember, your fear is just an illusion showing you an assumed future based on an uncomfortable past. This blueprint will guide you in stepping decisively out of your comfort zone, that familiar but often stagnant space where real growth seldom occurs, and into the arena of your potential. It will equip you to build the life you were not just meant to live, but the life you were destined to live, a life aligned with your deepest values and truest self.

You have been given one precious chance to experience and enjoy your life. Therefore, it is imperative that you make it count. You are inherently free to make any choice you desire, to forge any path you envision. However, you will never truly make the transformative choices you need to make until you fully grasp and internalize the immense power embedded within your own ability to choose. The path to living the life you were always destined for, the life of purpose and fulfillment you instinctively crave, begins right now, in this very moment. Yes, time is a finite and perishable resource. Time is running out.

Island of One: Born Different. Build to Thrive

PART I

Discovering Your Sovereign Territory

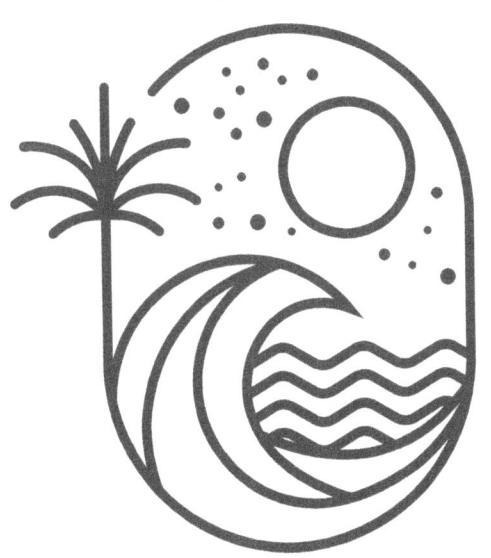

CHAPTER I

Discovering Your Sovereign Territory

"The concept, as I've come to understand it, transcends the mere feeling of being set apart. It delves into a core, unshakeable truth about the human condition: you are responsible for all of your choices and all of your opportunities."

So, you've arrived on your island. And trust me, it's not the kind with umbrella drinks, poolside service, and an endless supply of tiny paper umbrellas. Nope. This island—your personal island—is a bit more... rustic. Think less resort, more DIY survival adventure. It's the one you've been building, brick by sometimes-stubborn brick, ever since you first figured out how to tie your shoelaces (or, in my case, invented a highly sophisticated, one-handed knot-tying system that looks suspiciously like I'm doing a magic trick). You learn to adapt, right? And that's exactly what this journey is all about.

You Are Totally One-of-a-Kind (Seriously)

Here's the thing about you, and me, and everyone else walking around on this planet: you are unique. Like, truly unique. Nobody on this planet has your exact fingerprints, your crazy combination of quirks, your specific life story. You're a masterpiece, a singular blend of talents and weird habits.

And yet, if we're all so profoundly one-of-a-kind, why do we all seem to wrestle with the same nagging problems? Why do we find ourselves asking the same big-picture questions, hitting the same internal roadblocks, and battling the same familiar dragons of doubt and "I'll do it tomorrow" procrastination? It's almost as if, despite our wild individual landscapes, the human condition comes with a standard set of emotional potholes and intellectual dead ends.

This, my friend, is where we plant our flag. This is where you realize your island isn't just some random plot of land you happened to wash up on. This is your sovereign territory. And being sovereign means you're the one and only ruler. The undisputed, hopefully benevolent, dictator of everything that goes on within its borders.

Now, hold on. Before you start sketching plans for a moated castle and issuing royal decrees from a velvet throne, let's get crystal clear on what this "territory" actually is. It's not your overflowing bank account. It's not your neighbor's dog that apparently thinks 3 AM is prime barking time, or your favorite sports team's infuriating ability to snatch defeat from the jaws of victory. (Trust me, I know that frustration all too well!)

Your sovereign territory, my friend, is your mind. Your reactions. Your choices. It's that sacred, totally impenetrable space between what happens to you and what you decide to do about it. Think of it as your internal command center, the mission-critical hub of your entire being. And for way too long, too many of us have been letting a motley crew of unauthorized personnel run the show. We've got "Past Regrets" barging in, rearranging the mental furniture and pointing fingers; "Future Anxieties" fiddling with the alarm systems, making them blare at the most inconvenient moments; and the ever-present chorus of "What Will Other People Think?" shouting unsolicited advice from the sidelines, usually based on outdated or totally irrelevant data. It's like trying to pilot a fancy spaceship while a flock of agitated pigeons is trying to redecorate the cockpit with breadcrumbs and questionable nesting materials. Chaotic? Yep. Effective? Not a chance. Probably smells a bit, too.

The Invisible Fences on Your Island

And right there, among the pigeons and the well-meaning but ultimately distracting internal chatter, you'll find them: the invisible fences of your island. These aren't barbed wire or intimidating guard towers, but subtle, often self-imposed, psychological barriers. Maybe it's the fear of failure that keeps you from chasing that dream job, that audacious creative project, or even just trying a new recipe.

For me, growing up with one hand, these invisible fences were *super* real. It wasn't about physical barriers (though, trust me, there were those too—try opening a jar with one hand, or buttoning a shirt quickly!), but the sneaky internal whispers that told me what I "couldn't" or "shouldn't" do, especially in social situations. Could I ever *really* date someone if they saw my hand? This self-imposed barrier, born from a perceived difference, created a constant internal negotiation. It was exhausting.

Island of One: Born Different. Build to Thrive

My own specific "island" started forming even before I did. My dad, a true American hero who served 49 years in the Army, was exposed to Agent Orange in Vietnam. For those who don't know, Agent Orange was a pesticide used back in the 60s and 70s that, tragically, caused birth defects. I was a direct recipient of that. I was the fifth of five kids, but the only one born differently—without fingers on my left hand.

Growing up, my constant internal refrain was, "Why is everything different?" The world just wasn't designed for someone like me, and society wasn't shy about pointing that out. Oh, the names I was called! "One-handed monkey" was a popular one, often delivered with a sneer or a cruel giggle in the schoolyard. These experiences, man, they built invisible fences of fear around me, especially when it came to acceptance and belonging. I spent a huge chunk of my early life, particularly my teenage and dating years, trying to perfect "the art of hiding it." I mean, I would go on dates, spend time with women, and they wouldn't even know I had one hand because I was so ridiculously good at concealment. I'd keep it tucked in my pocket, or casually behind my back, always aware of its position. The more I hid, the more a fleeting sense of comfort would wash over me. But it was a comfort built on a lie, right? A hidden part of myself, tucked away and unseen. It was a constant effort, a full-on performance just to fit into a world that often felt totally unwelcoming to anyone different.

Then there was Halloween. Oh, Halloween was a whole *different* story entirely! For one glorious night, I could finally be cool. I had a prosthetic hook, just like Captain Hook. Suddenly, the very thing I spent all year trying to conceal and make disappear became my absolute superpower. Kids would crowd around, "Whoa, look what you've got! That's awesome! Can I go trick-or-treating with *him* and get more candy?" And you know what? I did. I got all the candy in the world you could possibly imagine, because everyone wanted to be friends with the guy with the cool hook. That hook, that symbol of a "difference" I usually hid, made me the "macaroni and the cheese ball." It was a stark, almost hilarious, contrast to my everyday reality. This brief taste of freedom on Halloween just screamed how much effort I was pouring into conforming, and how heavily those invisible fences—built from others' perceptions and my own internalized fears—weighed on my daily choices. It was a peek into what it felt like to be accepted, even celebrated, for my uniqueness, instead of being judged by it. A powerful lesson, even if I didn't fully grasp it then. It was a stark reminder of the energy I spent hiding, and the joy that could come from embracing who I was.

Or maybe it's the quiet, insidious weight of past experiences—a betrayal, a significant setback, a harsh criticism—subtly shaping your present decisions, keeping you from stepping too far out of line. Then there's that comfortable routine, that familiar groove that, over time, has subtly become a cage, offering a sense of security while simultaneously suffocating your growth and potential. These are the unwritten rules, the unspoken limitations, the silent agreements you've made with yourself or absorbed from the world around you, dictating where you can and cannot roam.

The Not-So-Fun Truth

You might be asking yourself, and maybe you've asked it a million times in the quiet of the night, staring at the ceiling, "Why don't I just *do* the things I know I should? Why don't I tackle those tasks I know I *must*? Why don't I just live the life I *dream* about?" It's a question that keeps more than a few of us up, silently judging our life choices, and occasionally wishing we had a magic remote control to fast-forward to a better version of ourselves.

Maybe it's plain old fear. That primal, knot-in-your-stomach sensation that whispers "danger!" whenever you even *think* about trying something new or challenging. Or a stubborn belief that you just *can't* do it, a deep-seated conviction that you lack the talent, the smarts, or the sheer gumption. The lingering ghost of your past, like a phantom limb, can still ache and dictate your movements. Financial constraints can feel like concrete walls, blocking every path. A perceived lack of support from your tribe can just sap your motivation. Inconvenient circumstances, anything from a broken washing machine to a global pandemic, can derail even the best intentions. Or (let's be brutally honest for a sec, just between us) maybe it's just plain laziness, that alluring siren song of the couch and Netflix. These are the relentless currents we all find ourselves paddling against, often without even realizing the immense strength we actually possess to navigate them.

Here's the inconvenient truth: we often let our circumstances, our past, our promises (especially those made to others, which can feel binding even when they no longer serve us), and everyone else's opinions literally *pave the way* for the choices we make. We outsource our decision-making, trading personal agency for perceived ease or social acceptance. In a very real sense, we become slaves to our own ambitions—or, perhaps more accurately, to our *lack* of ambition, settling for a quiet existence when our spirit is screaming for vibrancy. It just *feels* easier to merely exist, to float along with the tide, than to truly thrive, to deliberately paddle against it and steer towards a chosen destination.

But here's the crucial turning point: this feeling of isolation, this sense of being adrift on your own unique landmass, battling unseen currents, is a profoundly shared human experience. Every single person you meet, beneath their polished exterior, has their own set of invisible fences, their own internal pigeons, and their own nagging questions about unfulfilled potential. You're not the only one feeling those headwinds; you are part of a vast, unspoken human collective. Recognizing this shared journey is the very first, most empowering step toward true connection, and ultimately, toward liberating yourself from the shackles of self-doubt and external influence.

Welcome to Your Sovereign Territory!

The profound, sometimes startling (and occasionally knee-buckling) truth is this: ultimately, you are responsible for all of your choices and all of your opportunities. I know, I know. That first jolt of accountability can feel less like a gentle nudge and more like a sumo wrestler's embrace. It feels heavy, a bit overwhelming, almost like being handed the keys to a vast, complex machine you didn't even know you owned. Because if *you're* responsible, it means you can't blame your boss for your stagnant career, your ex for your current emotional baggage, the person who cut you off in traffic for your bad mood, or even that particularly insistent piece of lint that decided to cling to your favorite shirt all day and mock your attempts at tidiness.

But here's the magic trick: once you truly let that responsibility sink in, once you acknowledge that *you*—and only you—are the captain of your inner ship, that initial weight transforms into something exhilarating. It transforms into amazing freedom, a boundless sense of possibility. Because suddenly, you're not just a passenger, tossed about by life's unpredictable currents, merely reacting to whatever washes ashore. You're the one charting the course, unfurling the sails, and deciding where to drop anchor.

For me, being born with one hand could have been a reason to constantly blame "circumstance." Instead, it forced me to figure out how to adapt, how to tie those shoelaces, how to live fully. That forced innovation, that radical responsibility, was my first taste of true freedom. Every purposeful thought, every brave (or even slightly nervous) action, every little way you interpret the endless parade of life's events—it all stems from your own inherent power to act, a power that has always resided within you, waiting to be fully recognized and unleashed.

So, welcome to your sovereign territory. It might not have white sand beaches, but it has something far more valuable: absolute, unadulterated potential, stretching out beneath an infinite sky. Now, let's grab a map (the one we're drawing together, page by page, filled with strategies and insights) and start exploring. Because the most exciting part of this journey isn't just discovering the land; it's actively building the life you were always destined to live, right here, on your very own, perfectly unique island. And trust me, it's going to be an adventure.

CHAPTER II: Seizing the Helm of Your Life.

CHAPTER II

Seizing the Helm of Your life

"This reality of being an 'Island of One' by birth, I came to understand, meant I was designed to overcome everything."

The journey to your "Island of One" is about discovering your sovereign territory—that unique landscape of your life shaped by your circumstances, challenges, and perceived differences. You can move beyond a sense of isolation to a profound understanding of radical self-responsibility and the inherent power of choice. It is time to take charge of your life. Think of it: instead of just going along for the ride, you get to be the captain, steering your ship through whatever rough seas come your way. You need to spot those crucial moments when you need to make a decision, and understand that you're built to weather any storm.

Storms Can Either Capsize You or Reveal Your Strength

Life has a way of presenting us with moments that shake us to our core, jolting us from the comfortable rhythms of routine. My father, a man who truly loved seeking wisdom and unique perspectives, was instrumental in shaping how I understood these profound shifts. He introduced me to the words of ancient philosophers, like Epictetus, who in the 1st century AD, wisely observed: *"Man is not disturbed by things but the view in which he takes of them."* This seemingly simple statement carries immense weight, suggesting that our suffering often stems not from the event itself, but from our interpretation and reaction to it. My Dad had a remarkable way of distilling complex philosophical ideas into practical life lessons, always finding someone or something that could truly shed a new light on how to see the world, especially when it felt dark or overwhelming.

He shared with me about a thinker who had a very clear understanding of how people are fundamentally shaped by their experiences. Sociologist Morris Massey eloquently labeled these as "Significant Emotional Events" (SEEs)—experiences so potent they have the power to etch themselves indelibly into our psyche, profoundly shaping our core beliefs, values, and the subsequent choices we make. Massey posited a powerful truth: much of who we become is solidified by a certain age unless we encounter one of these transformative moments. These SEEs are the true storms of life, not mere passing showers. They can be sudden and violent, like a squall appearing unexpectedly on a calm horizon, threatening to capsize everything in an instant. Or they can be prolonged gales that relentlessly test our endurance, wearing down our defenses over time. They aren't always negative; an SEE can be a moment of intense loss, like the unexpected death of a loved one that forces a re-evaluation of life's fragility. It can be a profound business failure, the kind that rips away not just finances but also a sense of identity and competence. It can be an unexpected crisis, a health scare or a natural disaster that shatters illusions of control. Conversely, an SEE can also be a moment of overwhelming joy, a revelation that shifts our perspective entirely, like the birth of a child that instantly reorders all priorities, or a spiritual awakening that unveils a new purpose. The common thread is their intensity; they are moments too powerful to ignore, forcing a reckoning and demanding a shift in our internal landscape.

Think of a businessperson facing the crushing weight of bankruptcy, as I, too, have endured – not once, but twice in my career. Each instance was a descent into an abyss of self-doubt and despair, a feeling akin to being "smaller than an enigma." It was a profound sense of failure, a piercing awareness that I had somehow fallen out of sync with "society's pulse," a rhythm that seemed to demand perpetual success and upward momentum. The world, it felt, was moving forward, vibrant and thriving, while I was trapped in a still, desolate pocket, the echoes of my ambitions now hollow and mocking. The dreams I had nurtured, the risks I had bravely taken, now lay shattered around me, each fragment a painful reminder of promises unfulfilled and opportunities lost. It wasn't just the financial ruin that gnawed at my spirit, but the crushing blow to my identity, the feeling that I had betrayed not only myself but the expectations of those who had believed in my vision. In those dark moments, the weight of judgment, real or imagined, was almost unbearable, a constant companion whispering doubts and accusations.

Those were SEEs, moments where the storm threatened to capsize me entirely, leaving me feeling absolutely minuscule, like a tiny speck of dust in the vastness of the universe. It was a crushing sense of failure, not just professionally, but personally. Or consider the family from Italy at Checkpoint Charlie, gunned down for a simple misjudgment. For their loved ones, and perhaps even for young witnesses like myself and my father who arrived shortly after, that event could have been a deeply impactful SEE, shaping views on safety, authority, and the fragility of life in ways that stick with you forever.

SEEs aren't always grand or dramatic in the eyes of the world, but they are always significant to the individual experiencing them. Losing a cherished job after years of dedication can be an SEE, forcing a re-evaluation of identity and security. The end of a long-term relationship can feel like a personal earthquake, an SEE that reshapes your understanding of love and companionship. A sudden, serious health diagnosis can be an SEE that starkly reorders your priorities. Even positive events, like the birth of a child or a profound spiritual awakening, can be SEEs, fundamentally altering your life's trajectory and your perception of your place in the world.

The critical thing about these storms is not their occurrence—for storms are an inevitable part of any voyage—but their outcome. They hold a dual potential: they can capsize you, leaving you adrift in a sea of despair, fear, and limiting beliefs. Or, they can reveal your innate strength, forcing you to dig deep, to adapt, to learn, and to ultimately emerge more resilient and self-aware. The storm itself is a neutral force; its impact is determined by the captain's response. It's like the weather itself isn't good or bad, it just *is*. How you prepare for it and what you do during it makes all the difference.

The Pivotal Moment: Recognizing Your Power to Choose Your Response, Regardless of the Circumstance

Every Significant Emotional Event, every storm, brings with it a pivotal moment. This is the juncture where the path diverges. It's the point where, consciously or unconsciously, a choice is made—

a choice not about the event itself, for often we have no control over the storms that arise, but about our response to it. As I've emphasized, "Life can change if you make different choices." This is the heart of seizing the helm.

You are free to make any choice you want. But you will never make the choices you need—the transformative, empowering choices—until you understand the power inherent in your ability to make a choice. When faced with adversity, the default human reaction can often be one of fear, anger, or helplessness. We might feel like victims of circumstance, tossed about by waves we cannot control. And in that feeling, we often cede our power.

But the pivotal moment offers a different path. It's the recognition, however faint at first, that even amidst the most chaotic tempest, a sliver of agency remains. You can choose your thoughts. You can choose your attitude. You can choose your actions. "No matter what happened, you were there," I tell audiences. No matter how difficult, you were present, and in that presence lies the seed of choice. That presence means you have a say in what happens next, even if it's just how you respond internally.

Imagine the individual who loses their job. That SEE is undeniably painful. The pivotal moment arrives: do they choose to see this as a confirmation of their inadequacy, a path to prolonged unemployment and bitterness? Or do they choose to see it as an unexpected detour, an opportunity to reassess their passions, learn new skills, and perhaps embark on a more fulfilling career they never would have considered otherwise? The circumstance is the same; the chosen response dictates the journey forward.

Consider someone who receives a frightening medical diagnosis. The fear is real, the uncertainty immense. But the pivotal moment is there: the choice to surrender to despair, or the choice to fight, to seek knowledge, to find support, to live each remaining day with purpose and intention, regardless of the prognosis. Helen Keller, blind and deaf, chose not to be defined by her limitations but to become a beacon of inspiration. Stephen Hawking, diagnosed with ALS, chose to expand our understanding of the universe. Jim Abbott, born without a right hand, chose to become a Major League Baseball pitcher. Each faced monumental SEEs, and each made a pivotal choice about their response. They didn't let the storm define their destination.

This power of choice is not about denying pain or suppressing emotions. It's about acknowledging the reality of the storm while simultaneously recognizing that you, the captain, still have your hands on the helm. Your fear, so often, "is just an illusion showing you an assumed future based on an uncomfortable past." When you realize this, you begin to take back your power from that fear. It's like seeing the wizard behind the curtain – once you know it's not real, it loses its power.

A Conscious Decision to Redefine Your Reality

For me, a defining SEE and a pivotal moment arrived early, on a dusty kickball field in second grade. As I shared in the introduction, a classmate, in a moment of unfiltered childhood cruelty, called me a "one-handed monkey." The words were a direct hit, aimed squarely at my most visible difference, my "island." The pain was acute, searing. That was the storm. It felt like my young world was crumbling right there in the dirt.

In that instant, I could have retreated. I could have allowed his words to become my truth, a label that would define and limit me. I could have let that SEE capsize my young spirit, leading to a life of hiding, shame, and accepted limitation. Many people, when faced with such direct and painful confrontations with their perceived differences, make such a choice, often unconsciously, internalizing the negative judgments of others. It's easy to just fold and disappear.

But something else happened. Fueled by a potent mix of pain, indignation, and the echo of my mother's unwavering belief—"You're more than what you were born as"—a different choice sparked within me. It wasn't a calm, reasoned decision at that age, but it was a decision nonetheless. It was a surge of what I can only describe as "kickball fury," a white-hot determination not just to prove that kid wrong, but to prove the entire world wrong if necessary.

That was my pivotal moment. Instead of succumbing to the humiliation, I chose to fight back, not with fists, but with a fierce resolve to meet every challenge, to defy every expectation, and to redefine what was possible for someone like me. That day, the pain of the taunt didn't disappear, but it was transformed. It became fuel. I made a conscious decision that my reality would not be dictated by the ignorance of others or by the apparent limitations of my physical form. I would be the one to define my capabilities and my worth. This SEE, this verbal assault, became the catalyst for a lifelong commitment to overcoming, to adapting, and to proving that my "island" was not a place of deficit but a unique landscape that would forge unique strengths. It set me on a path to actively shape my own destiny.

Understanding That Your Unique Makeup Is Not a Mistake

That kickball incident and the choice I made in its wake solidified a truth I believe applies to every single one of us: our unique

CHAPTER II: Seizing the Helm of Your Life.

makeup, our personal "island" with all its specific challenges and differences, is not a mistake. It is not a cosmic error or a sign of deficiency. It is, in fact, an inherent design for overcoming. As I came to understand, "This reality of being an 'Island of One' by birth, meant I was designed to overcome everything."

The world is not designed for someone with one hand. Every day presented, and still presents, puzzles to solve: tying shoes, cutting food, playing sports, riding a motorcycle, flying an airplane. Each of these could have been a reason to say, "I can't." But the inherent design for overcoming whispers, "How can I?" It forces innovation, adaptation, and a level of resilience that might otherwise lie dormant. I had to figure out how to play the guitar by buying a left-handed one and teaching myself, strumming with the hand that has only one fingernail and fingering chords with my "rhythm" hand. It works. I had to work with a team to invent a device to fly a plane from the standard left seat, and before that, I bought a plane and re-engineered it to fly from the right. This wasn't about stubbornness; it was about answering the call of that inherent design. "God already gave what you need to do what He wants you to do," as I often say. The tools might look different, the path might be unconventional, but the capacity to overcome is built-in. It's like having a custom-built car for a unique terrain – it's designed to handle *that* specific challenge.

This principle isn't exclusive to those with visible physical differences. Someone who struggles with a learning disability might develop extraordinary compensatory skills in other areas, like exceptional creativity or empathetic abilities. An individual who grows up in poverty might cultivate a resourcefulness and tenacity that becomes their greatest asset in business and in life. A person who battles anxiety might develop a profound self-awareness and a deep capacity for compassion towards others'

45

struggles. As the Roman philosopher Seneca observed, "Every new beginning comes from some other beginning's end." Your "island"—whether it's a physical difference, a challenging past, a difficult personality trait you're working to manage, or a set of circumstances that seem to put you at a disadvantage—is the very training ground that forges the skills, perspectives, and strengths you need to thrive. The perceived disadvantage, the thing that makes you feel separate or ill-equipped, often compels the development of precisely those qualities that lead to extraordinary achievement and profound personal growth. The key is to stop seeing your island as a prison and start seeing it as your unique, purpose-built vessel for navigating the seas of life.

The act of seizing the helm, therefore, begins with this profound shift in perspective. It's about recognizing the SEEs in your life as opportunities for pivotal choices. It's about claiming your power to respond, regardless of the storm. And it's about embracing your inherent design, understanding that whatever makes up your "Island of One" is not a barrier to your success, but the very blueprint for it. You are not just meant to survive the voyage; you are designed to captain it with courage, creativity, and an unyielding belief in your ability to reach your chosen destination.

PART II

The 7 Keys to Thriving on Your Is land

CHAPTER III

C is for Clarity *(Your Plan)*
Charting A Deliberate Course

"A plan is the antidote to this reactive existence. It is the conscious act of saying, 'This is where I am going, and this is how I intend to get there."

Designing Your Island's Deliberate Plan

Hey friend, welcome to the 'C' in our COMPASS System: **Clarity**! This is where we really get to dig in, get super clear on what you envision for your life, and gently start mapping out your path forward. Because, honestly, even the coolest adventurer needs a treasure map, right? You wouldn't just hop on a ship and sail aimlessly across the ocean, would you?

We've already been on quite a journey together, haven't we? We've explored your incredible, innate Gifts, found ways to truly master your Time, and even started reclaiming your Past, transforming those stories. Each one of those steps, those 'keys,' has helped us unlock a deeper understanding of just how powerful and capable you truly are.

Now, we're at such an exciting point: taking all that incredible understanding and turning it into something real, something you can actually touch and move towards. The first step is all about *Charting Your Course* – shifting from just knowing what's possible to deliberately building your island's blueprint for thriving. Think of it like this: without a clear path, even the most amazing 'aha!' moments can just fade away, like morning mist. But with a plan, those hopes can become a true direction and a path you're actually able to start walking. Yes, when I discovered this I found nothing but peace of mind.

Why a Plan is Absolutely Essential

You know that old saying, *"If you fail to plan, you are planning to fail!"*? While it sounds a bit stern, there's a lot of truth to it, especially when we're talking about truly transforming your life. So many of us, myself included at times, just kind of float through our days. We react to whatever pops up, get pushed around by external stuff, and then wonder why we never quite land where we want to be. As I've often said, *"Most of us exist, but do not live."* It's like we let our days just *happen* to us, like a leaf gently drifting wherever the wind decides to blow. Living life from *"sleep-to-sleep."*

A plan, my friend, is the wonderful antidote to that reactive existence. It's the conscious, empowering act of saying, *'This is where I am going, and this is how I intend to get there.'*

Just think about any big thing you've ever wanted to do: build a cozy home, kickstart a new business, get a degree, or even just plan a truly memorable vacation. Would you ever jump into any of those without some sort of blueprint, a little business sketch, or a fun itinerary? To do that would probably invite a whole lot of chaos, wasted energy, and let's be honest, likely some disappointment.

Your life – your very own "Island of One" – is probably the most significant project you'll ever undertake. With God as my secret judge, It absolutely deserves, no, **it *demands*** a deliberate plan. As Antoine de Saint-Exupéry beautifully put it, *"A goal without a plan is just a wish."* And a wish, while lovely and full of potential, rarely gets you very far on its own, does it?

So, why is having a plan so incredibly crucial? Because it:

- **Brings Clarity and Focus:** It gently nudges you to define what you *truly* want, cutting through all that foggy uncertainty. It's like switching on a powerful lighthouse beam in the darkness, showing you the way.
- **Creates a Gentle Roadmap:** It takes those big, sometimes daunting aspirations and breaks them down into sweet, manageable steps, showing you the way forward. You don't have to see the *entire* path, just the next few friendly steps.
- **Lets You See Your Progress:** It gives you little markers to track your journey, places to celebrate those wonderful milestones, and moments to make necessary adjustments. There's really nothing quite like the satisfaction of crossing something off a list, is there?
- **Builds That Inner Sense of Accountability:** A written plan is like a quiet promise you make to yourself. And if you choose to share it with a trusted friend, that promise often feels even stronger. It's your way of saying, *"I'm serious about this, and I'm ready!"*
- **Helps You Build Momentum:** Each small win you achieve, guided by your plan, builds a quiet confidence and fuels you

CHAPTER III: C is for Clarity (Your Plan) Charting a Deliberate Course

for the next step. It's like a happy snowball rolling downhill, picking up speed as it goes.

As I've learned, often the hard way through business ventures that soared and then, well, crashed (and trust me, there were more than a few tumbles – I've gone bankrupt not once, but twice!), and through personal trials that tested every fiber of my being, "if you could do everything with the information you had in the past, you would have done it already by now." This isn't an indictment of your past efforts or your intelligence; it's a fundamental truth about growth and change.

Sometimes we get a bit stuck when we unconsciously operate solely on old information or familiar patterns, almost expecting different results from the same inputs. A true plan, then, isn't just about diligently repeating past actions that might have offered limited success or even led to a stumble. It's a dynamic, exciting process of consciously weaving in new knowledge—that hard-won wisdom from your own experiences, those fresh insights you've gained from learning and observation (like the gems from exploring your Gifts, Time, and Past in our previous chats)—and, crucially, a renewed, conscious intention to forge a new path. It's a path that's informed by your past but absolutely not shackled to it. It's about gently acknowledging that what got you *here* won't necessarily get you *there*, and having the quiet courage to design a strategy that beautifully reflects your evolved understanding and your deepest aspirations.

Beyond Vague Hopes: Translating Desires into Concrete, Actionable Goals

"I want to be happy." "I want to be successful." "I want a better life." These are such common, lovely sentiments, full of aspiration. But as a plan? They're just not quite effective. They're wonderful, vague hopes, but not yet actionable goals. To truly chart your course, we need to gently translate these desires into something concrete, something you can truly aim for and really work towards.

Remember those things that "make you sing, dream, and cry," which we explored earlier when we talked about your purpose? Those are the beautiful raw materials for your goals. They are the deeply personal desires that truly ignite your soul.

So, let's chat: what does "happy" *specifically* look like for you? Does it mean more precious quality time with your family? Perhaps pursuing a creative passion that truly makes your heart sing? Or maybe living in a particular environment that feels just right? For me, "happy" is definitely spending time with my wife Sofia and our daughters, truly present and connected, soaking in every moment.

And how do *you* define "successful"? Is it about financial abundance, creating a sense of security? Making a significant, positive impact in your community? Or perhaps achieving mastery in a chosen field that you adore? For me, it's absolutely about making an impact, sharing what I've learned, and finding ways to give back.

What tangible changes would truly make your life feel "better"? Improved health and vitality? Stronger, more meaningful relationships? A deeper sense of peace of mind?

The process of planning gently forces you to drill down into these generalities and uncover the specific outcomes you truly seek. This is where those wonderful, vague hopes begin to softly transform into the solid building blocks of your very own "Thrive Plan."

CHAPTER III: C is for Clarity (Your Plan) Charting a Deliberate Course

Evolution from Reactive Adaptation to Proactive Life

For a significant portion of my formative years, especially as I wrestled with the inherent complexities of being born with a single hand, my main strategy was always about reactive adaptation. Life constantly threw challenges my way—the intricate fingering needed to play a guitar, the formidable task of lifting substantial weights, the precise maneuvering demanded by flying an airplane—and each time, I just had to figure out a solution. This often meant inventing a unique device or developing a highly individualized, unconventional technique.

While undeniably a testament to my knack for problem-solving, this approach remained mostly reactive. My actions were a direct response to limitations imposed by the outside world, or by what I felt were my immediate needs. It was kind of like being in a perpetual state of firefighting, where each new obstacle was a blaze that demanded immediate attention and a makeshift extinguisher, rather than a concerted effort to build a comprehensive and resilient fire-prevention system that could preemptively mitigate potential conflagrations. The cycle was relentless: encounter a barrier, then expend mental and physical energy to get around it, only to find another barrier waiting just beyond. This constant state of improvisation, while effective in the moment, lacked the foresight and systemic planning that would later become a cornerstone of a more proactive and empowering philosophy for me.

The shift towards proactive life design really came with a deeper understanding of choice and purpose. It wasn't just about overcoming specific obstacles anymore; it was about consciously deciding what kind of life I truly wanted to build, what impact I wanted to make, and then designing a plan to achieve that. This wasn't merely about setting goals, but about cultivating a *mindset* of intentional creation, where every decision, every step, was aligned with a larger, personal vision. My business bankruptcies were painful but incredibly powerful teachers in the necessity of planning—not just financial planning, but *life* planning. The sting of those failures forced a profound re-evaluation, not just of business models, but of my entire approach to living. I realized that simply reacting to market forces or immediate pressures wasn't sustainable; it was like trying to patch a leaky boat while still out at sea. I needed a robust vision, a flexible yet firm strategy, and deliberate, measured steps forward. These experiences taught me that true resilience comes not from avoiding falls, but from learning how to get back up, wiser and with a clearer map.

Running over 100 different companies throughout my career has been an extraordinary school of hard knocks, each venture a unique lesson in iteration and strategic planning. I've been a "serial entrepreneur," as I call it, diving into everything from online advertising firms with offices in London and Australia, to a site helping people find money (RaisingMoney.com, which, spoiler alert, didn't quite raise money for *me*, ironically!), to even creating a vending company for children selling diapers in malls. Some failed spectacularly, like "We Should Chat," where I learned a huge lesson about genuinely understanding market need and user engagement – sometimes, a good idea on paper doesn't translate into what people actually want to *do*. Others, like the diaper vending machines, were successful enough to be sold off, teaching me about scaling, operational efficiency, and knowing when to pivot or exit. Each one, regardless of outcome, was less a failure and more a tuition payment for an invaluable education. They taught me that sheer effort isn't enough without a coherent plan, and that flexibility within that plan is paramount. You truly need to "start with the end in mind," as I often say, because even if a venture fails, you don't lose the foundational knowledge; instead, you learn how to pivot, how to adjust your sails, and how to build another boat if your current ship encounters rough waters. You emerge smarter, tougher, and significantly more strategic, ready for the next adventure.

This evolution is beautifully mirrored in the journey this book invites you to take. You've identified your gifts, confronted your time robbers, and begun to reframe your past. Now, instead of simply reacting to your island's existing landscape, you're going to become its deliberate architect. You're moving from saying, "This is what my island is," to declaring, "This is what my island *will become*." As Peter Drucker famously stated, "The best way to predict the future is to create it." And that, my friend, is exactly what we're doing right now.

Actionable Strategies: Building Your "Thrive Plan"

Charting your course requires more than just good intentions; it truly requires a practical framework. Here's a step-by-step approach to creating your personalized "Thrive Plan" – something that feels right for *you*.

A Step-by-Step Guide to Creating Your Personalized **"Thrive Plan"**

1. **Revisit Your Core, Gently:**
   - **Your Eulogy and Mission Statement:** Take a moment to remember what you defined as most important, what you want to be remembered for, and your core purpose. These are your ultimate guiding stars, the bedrock of your "Thrive Plan." What kind of beautiful legacy do you want to leave on

your island?
- **Your Gifts:** Gently remind yourself of your innate strengths. Your plan should absolutely lean into these gifts, making your journey easier and more enjoyable. Why swim against the current when you can use your strongest stroke?
- **Your Values:** What principles are absolutely non-negotiable for you? Your plan must align with your core values to be truly sustainable and fulfilling. If integrity is a core value, your plan shouldn't involve anything shady, no matter how tempting it might seem.

2. **Define Your Key Life Areas:** Most people find it helpful to gently break their life down into manageable areas. Common examples include:

- Health & Wellbeing (physical, mental, emotional)
- Career & Finances
- Relationships (family, friends, romantic)
- Personal Growth & Learning
- Contribution & Spirituality (how you give back, your connection to something larger)
- Fun & Recreation

Choose the areas that resonate most with you right now. What aspects of your life truly feel like they need your loving attention and growth at this moment?

3. **Brainstorm Your Vision for Each Area:** For each life area you've identified, allow yourself to envision your *ideal* state. Don't censor yourself – let your imagination truly run wild!

- What would thriving in this area look and feel like one year from now? Three years? Five years? Paint a vivid, beautiful picture.
- If there were absolutely no limitations, what would you truly want to achieve or experience? Forget what seems "realistic"

for a moment; just allow yourself to dream.

4. Translate Vision into S.M.A.R.T. Goals: Now, this is a point that I most certainly did not invent – it's been spoken about time and time again, and for good reason! This is where our gentle dreams meet real-world action. For each life area, let's set 1-3 key goals using the S.M.A.R.T. criteria. It's a wonderful way to make things clear:

- **S - Specific:** Let's clearly define what you want to accomplish. What exactly, why, who's involved, where, which?
    - *Vague:* "Get healthier."
    - *Specific:* "I want to lose 15 pounds and complete a 5k run to improve my cardiovascular health and energy levels by October 31st." See the wonderful difference? It's so much clearer!
- **M - Measurable:** How will you track your progress and know when you've lovingly achieved your goal?
    - *Not Measurable:* "Improve my finances."
    - *Measurable:* "I will increase my monthly savings by $500 and reduce credit card debt by $2,000 within six months." You can actually see those numbers moving, which is so satisfying!
- **A - Achievable (or Action-Oriented):** Is the goal realistic given your current resources and what's going on in your life? What gentle actions are required? It should stretch you a little, but not be so far out of reach that it feels disheartening.
    - *Potentially Unachievable:* "Become a millionaire in one year starting from zero." (Unless you win the lottery, which isn't quite a plan!)
    - *Achievable:* "I will develop a detailed business plan and secure initial funding for my startup within nine months." That's a stretch, but it's absolutely doable.

- **R - Relevant:** Does this goal truly align with your overall vision, your values, and your mission? Does it genuinely matter to you? Is it the right time for this specific step?
    - *Potentially Irrelevant:* Setting a goal to learn rock climbing if your core values are around quiet intellectual pursuits and family time, unless there's a deeper connection you've identified that truly makes your heart sing.
    - *Relevant:* "I will dedicate 5 hours per week to writing my novel (this aligns beautifully with my creative fulfillment goal) to complete the first draft in one year." This clearly ties back to your heartfelt purpose.
- **T - Time-bound:** Let's set a specific deadline or timeframe for achieving the goal. This creates a gentle sense of urgency and helps prevent procrastination. Without a deadline, a goal can sometimes just remain a lovely dream with no gentle push.
    - *Not Time-bound:* "Learn Spanish."
    - *Time-bound:* "I will achieve conversational fluency in Spanish by enrolling in a course and practicing daily for one year, with a target of holding a 15-minute conversation by December 31st." Now that's a wonderful challenge you can truly plan for!

5. **Break Down Goals into Action Steps:** For each S.M.A.R.T. goal, let's identify the specific, gentle actions you need to take to achieve it. What are the very first steps? What are the weekly or monthly tasks that will move you forward?

- *Goal:* "Lose 15 pounds and complete a 5k run in six months."
- *Action Steps:*
    - Consult a nutritionist for a meal plan (Week 1).
    - Join a gym and schedule three 30-minute workouts per week (Week 1).
    - Begin a couch-to-5k running program (Week 1).

- Track food intake daily.
- Weigh in weekly to monitor progress.

You get the idea, right? Break it down until each step feels wonderfully manageable and clear.

6. **Schedule Your Actions:** A plan without scheduled action steps is, well, just a wish list. Let's lovingly integrate these action steps into your daily and weekly schedule. Treat these appointments with yourself as seriously as you would an appointment with your most important client or your doctor. If we don't schedule it, it probably won't happen, and we want to make sure it does!

7. **Build in Accountability and Adaptability:**

- **Accountability:**
    - Self-Accountability: Regularly review your plan (daily, weekly, monthly). Track your progress. Be gentle but honest with yourself.
    - External Accountability: Consider sharing your goals with a trusted friend, mentor, coach, or family member who can offer support and help keep you gently on track. Sometimes, just knowing someone else is cheering you on (or checking in!) is enough.
- **Adaptability:** Life happens, doesn't it? Your plan is a beautiful guide, not a rigid prison. Be prepared to review and adjust your plan as circumstances gently shift or as you learn more about yourself and what truly matters. An effective plan is a living, breathing document. Don't be afraid to reassess, recalibrate, or even change course if a goal no longer serves your highest good. The aim is always progress, not perfection in adhering to an outdated plan. It's like navigating a ship: you have a destination, but you adjust for the winds and tides, always moving forward.

Your **"Thrive Plan"** is your personal declaration of intent, a beautiful blueprint you design for building the life you truly desire on your unique Island of One. It gently transforms you from a passive observer into the active, deliberate creator of your own wonderful reality. The journey of a thousand miles begins with a single step, and your plan beautifully illuminates those first crucial steps, and all the ones that follow. So, grab your compass, draw your map, and let's set sail on this amazing adventure together!

CHAPTER IV
O is for Ownership *(Your Gifts)*
Unearthing Your Innate Gifts

"God already gave what you need to do what He wants to do."

The Hidden Treasures of Your Island

When we hear the word "gifts," our minds often quickly jump to the usual suspects – an extraordinary singing voice that could fill a stadium, breathtaking athletic prowess, or perhaps a genius-level knack for complex mathematics. And while, yes, these are absolutely gifts, the treasures hidden on your unique "Island of One" are far, far broader, much deeper, and often, surprisingly, forged in the very fires of your life's experiences, especially your toughest challenges.

Beyond Conventional Talents

To truly thrive, to genuinely step into your fullest potential, we need to gently expand our understanding of what actually counts as a "gift." So, let's think beyond the stage lights or the roar of a stadium crowd. Your innate gifts include the profound resilience that allows you to bounce back from adversity, that quiet spark of creativity that helps you find fresh, novel solutions when everyone else is stuck, the deep well of empathy that connects you so powerfully to others, and the absolutely unique perspectives that have been shaped by your individual journey. These aren't just pleasant traits you happen to have; they are potent, deeply ingrained tools, the inherent resources you possess within you to navigate life's beautiful, sometimes messy, complexities.

As I've said before, so many of us walk through life feeling like we're operating from a place of lack, constantly searching for something external to complete us or solve our problems. We look outside, hoping to acquire what we believe is missing. But the profound truth, the liberating realization, is this: "you were born with everything you need to live a life of purpose and meaning." The most potent gifts are often those that aren't immediately obvious, the ones you may have innocently overlooked or even mistakenly perceived as weaknesses simply because they were born from struggle. They are the hidden treasures of your island, waiting patiently beneath the surface, just waiting to be excavated. And here's the kicker: you've been carrying this treasure map all along; you just didn't quite know it.

How Physical Difference Forced Innovation
From Perceived Limitation to Unveiled Strength

My personal island, as many of you know, was mapped out early in life by a visible physical difference. For far too long, the world around me—and at times, even I myself—became fixated on what was perceived to be missing. It was as if my identity was being defined by an absence rather than the wholeness of who I was.

The journey through childhood and adolescence was punctuated by constant, often subtle, challenges. Simple tasks that others took for granted – holding a pencil, tying a shoe, catching a ball – became complex puzzles for me to solve. It wasn't a question of if I could accomplish something, but rather how I could approach it differently, constantly innovating, adapting, and finding my own unique way to navigate a world that wasn't designed for my particular physicality. This constant need to adapt began to subtly hone a very powerful internal muscle: resourcefulness.

My mother, a woman whose every decision was imbued with a quiet strength and a wisdom forged in the crucible of life's unpredictable currents, once shared with me a memory from my infancy that remains indelibly etched in my consciousness. It was a moment of profound choice, a precipice upon which the very trajectory of my life teetered. As a baby, I was presented with a medical dilemma of an agonizing nature: an operation on my left hand. This procedure, she explained, held the promise of granting me a rudimentary functionality—the ability to form a claw or a basic grip, enabling me to hold objects, however clumsily, with that hand.

The sheer, monumental weight of that decision, even now, decades later, feels almost too immense to fully grasp. For a new mother, cradling a newborn in her arms, her heart a delicate balance of boundless hope and gnawing fear, to be confronted with such a profound medical choice must have been an agonizing ordeal of an almost unbearable intensity. This was not a fleeting consideration, a passing thought dismissed with a shrug; it was a lifetime of implications, a boundless array of potential futures, resting squarely upon her young shoulders. Every conceivable outcome, every divergent path my life might take, must have been meticulously weighed and reweighed in the hushed stillness of countless sleepless nights. The unspoken fears, the desperate

CHAPTER IV: O is for Ownership (Your Gifts) Unearthing Your Innate Gifts

prayers, the silent pleas for guidance—all must have swirled around her as she grappled with the enormity of what lay before her.

And yes, there exists within me a lingering, almost imperceptible whisper of curiosity: if I had undergone that operation, would my path have diverged? Would the subtle shift in my physical capabilities have rippled outward, altering the very fabric of my existence? Would I have gravitated towards different passions, embraced alternative challenges, or found myself living a life subtly reshaped by the presence of a more functional left hand? It is a natural, perhaps even inescapable, human inclination to dwell on the "what ifs," to trace the phantom threads of alternative destinies that life might have unspooled. We are, after all, creatures of curiosity, forever pondering the roads not taken.

However, the truth—a truth that has solidified with each passing year, each new experience, each challenge overcome—is this: I am profoundly, absolutely convinced that I would not have scaled the profound milestones, nor cultivated the deep understanding and insights, that I have painstakingly discovered, articulated, and laid bare within the very pages of this narrative. The myriad challenges I have faced, the ingenious adaptations I have been compelled to devise, and the singular, unique perspective that has blossomed as a direct consequence of my left hand's inherent limitations—these have been the forge in which the person I am today was tempered. These experiences have served as the crucibles, refining my resilience to an unbreakable strength, igniting the dormant embers of my creativity into a vibrant flame, and deepening the wellspring of my empathetic spirit to an immeasurable degree. The arduous, yet ultimately illuminating, journey I have embarked upon, shaped irrevocably by that early, pivotal decision, has, in the grand tapestry of my life, led me to a place of profound self-discovery, a richer and more nuanced appreciation for the intricate beauty of life's unpredictable currents, and an unshakeable sense of purpose.

Finding a Path to achieve what others take for granted

This early conditioning, a subtle yet pervasive influence, inexorably guided me down a path where external solutions became my default. I vividly recall the nascent stages of articulating this profound need to "build something for everything," a mantra that echoed through my early attempts to navigate a world seemingly designed for others. The physical challenges I faced, born from a congenital difference, weren't just obstacles; they were calls to innovation, albeit innovation rooted in a deep-seated belief that I was fundamentally lacking. It felt as though I was constantly trying to fit a square peg into a round hole, forever seeking the perfect external tool to compensate for what I perceived as an internal deficiency.

The profound turning point, a monumental realization of my innate gifts and capabilities, arrived when I began to fundamentally question this very approach. Why was I continually writing checks, pouring resources into these external fixes? The answer came in a moment of clarity, a revelation I've since shared widely: "Maybe, just maybe God already gave me everything that I need." This simple yet profound thought marked a monumental paradigm shift. It wasn't about adding to myself; it was about acknowledging and trusting what was already inherent. It was a shift from looking outward for solutions to turning inward for my true strengths.

This newfound perspective led to transformative actions, not just in my mindset but in my life. Instead of retrofitting myself to the airplane, trying to force my body into a standard cockpit configuration, I consciously re-engineered the airplane to suit me, learning to fly with proficiency and confidence from the right seat, leveraging my existing capabilities and natural right-handed dominance. My passion for music found expression as I learned to play the guitar, not in the conventional way most people do, but in my own unique fashion—a left-handed guitar played with a strumming and fretting style that was uniquely mine, a testament to what creativity can unlock. I discovered the exhilarating freedom of skiing without a pole, my balance and coordination adapting effortlessly to the slopes, proving that limitations can force elegant, simpler solutions. And golf? My "one hand," once a source of deep insecurity and a perceived limitation, truly transformed into the very catalyst for innovation and resourcefulness. I currently maintain a very respectable 18 handicap, and if you watch me play, you won't see any fancy devices or external aids. This so-called "limitation" didn't just force me to think outside the conventional box; it compelled me to find solutions that were authentically mine, stemming directly from my inherent abilities, showcasing how constraint can breed ingenious solutions.

Working out with weights

To engage in the rigorous discipline of strength training, an activity I craved for its promise of physical empowerment and the feeling of growing stronger, I meticulously engineered a specialized device. This wasn't a simple brace; it was a complex contraption that I would painstakingly strap on, twist, and tighten each time, a rigid extension that allowed me to securely grip weights. It transformed what was inherently difficult – the act of holding heavy dumbbells or barbells – into something marginally achievable, a constant test of my ingenuity and persistence.

At the same time, I faced the challenge of using workout

machines, which have such a vast diversity of grips and handles. I scoured stores, initially drawn to the weightlifting section, where I discovered a hook designed for deadlifting. It was a sturdy, seemingly practical device, offering a glimmer of hope. But what I didn't anticipate was the sheer variety of gym equipment grips. This one hook, while helpful for certain exercises, was far from a universal solution, leaving me frustrated on many machines. My quest for a truly adaptable tool led me to purchase over 30 different straps and hooks, each one a hopeful experiment, a testament to my determination to find a way to engage with the machines that others used so effortlessly. Each new strap was a gamble, a hope that this one would be the missing piece of the puzzle, allowing me to finally wrap my left hand around the myriad of bars and grips I encountered at the gym. It was a process of trial and error, a constant refinement of my approach, as I slowly but surely pieced together a system that allowed me to work out effectively, transforming my personal "island of one" into a space of active, physical engagement and growth. This persistent experimentation was itself a gift—the gift of unwavering commitment to a solution.

Trying to Surf or Swim

Swimming, a pursuit that offered moments of fleeting weightlessness and freedom, presented a unique hurdle. The absence of fingers meant I simply couldn't generate enough propulsion to swim effectively with both hands. It was a disheartening realization, watching others glide effortlessly while my own attempts felt like a struggle against the water itself. I vividly recall an attempt to learn surfing with my older brother, an endeavor that quickly devolved into a nightmare. I had invested in a longboard, a wetsuit, and all the necessary gear, envisioning mornings spent "hanging ten" and catching waves with ease. After all, living in Orange County, it felt almost genetically

CHAPTER IV: O is for Ownership (Your Gifts) Unearthing Your Innate Gifts

predetermined that I should be a surfer. However, the very first day in the water made it unequivocally clear: I would never achieve the necessary speed to catch a wave. The frustration was palpable, a stark reminder of the limitations I faced even in activities that promised liberation. Every paddle was a struggle against the water, a desperate attempt to compensate for what wasn't there. The dream of effortlessly gliding across the ocean's surface dissolved with each failed attempt, leaving behind only the cold reality of a body that, despite its will, could not conform to the demands of the sport in that conventional way.

The relentless pursuit of a natural connection with the ocean, once symbolized by the surfboard, eventually yielded to a more pragmatic, yet equally determined, endeavor: mastering the disciplined art of lap swimming. The inherent instability of surfing, a beautiful dance with an ever-changing canvas, proved too elusive with my particular challenges. Thus, my focus shifted from the vast, unpredictable expanse of the sea to the more controlled, albeit still demanding, environment of the swimming pool.

My initial attempts at traditional swimming were met with frustrating limitations. The natural rhythm and balance that seemed to come so effortlessly to others remained stubbornly out of reach. It was a disheartening realization, but one that ignited a spark of ingenuity. Rather than surrender to these physical constraints, I resolved to engineer a solution, a bespoke augmentation that would bridge the gap between my current capabilities and my aquatic aspirations.

The genesis of this device was born from a period of intense ideation and experimentation. I envisioned something that would not merely assist but would, in essence, extend my own physical reach and stability. The foundational component was a sturdy, adjustable strap, designed to be securely fastened around my left wrist. This strap served as the anchor for the more innovative element: a specially crafted paddle. This wasn't merely an off-the-shelf swimming aid; it was a carefully selected piece, chosen for its unique hydrodynamic properties and its capacity to provide the necessary leverage. I meticulously secured this paddle to the wrist strap, ensuring a firm, unyielding connection that would withstand the forces of propulsion through water.

The resulting contraption was, in its essence, a bespoke amalgamation of buoyant materials and hydrodynamic forms. It was a deliberate, almost sculptural, creation, meticulously designed to perform a singular, crucial function: to help me maintain balance and optimize propulsion in the water. It functioned as an external skeletal support, compensating for the innate lack of equilibrium that had previously hindered my progress. With this device, I could finally achieve a full, powerful stroke, an experience that had eluded me for so long. The water, once a chaotic, uncooperative medium, now responded to my efforts with a newfound grace.

And it worked. The sensation of gliding through the water, propelled by a stroke that felt complete and effective, was exhilarating. The device had unlocked a new dimension of aquatic movement, transforming a previously frustrating experience into one of genuine accomplishment. However, this triumph was not without its practical inconveniences. The device, while effective, was a cumbersome appendage. The ritual of strapping it on, ensuring its secure fit, and then having to manage its presence outside of the water, proved to be an unexpected burden. Each trip to the pool became an exercise not only in physical exertion but also in logistical preparation.

So, despite the undeniable success in finding a technical solution to my swimming challenges, the very practicality of that solution ultimately led to a difficult decision. The cumbersome nature of the device, the ongoing hassle of bringing it to and from the pool, eventually outweighed the benefits it offered. The initial spark of innovation, while leading to a functional solution, could not entirely overcome the friction of everyday use. And so, with a lingering sense of paradox—having found the answer, only to set it aside—I ultimately put my swimming aspirations on hold, focusing instead on other avenues where my natural adaptability could flourish more seamlessly.

Playing Golf

Golf, for me, was never just a pastime; it was a profound crucible where my competitive spirit was forged, a pursuit that demanded every ounce of ingenuity I possessed. The challenge, however, was significant. While my right hand could initiate a swing, the crucial power derived from the left hand, the ability to "pull through the stroke" with force and control, was absent. This deficit, this perceived gap in my physical capability, became the genesis of an obsessive quest: to engineer a solution, a custom-molded device that would bridge this gap and allow me to harness the full power of my swing.

The requirements were clear, yet daunting. The device had to be a seamless extension of my body, allowing me to connect my left hand to the club with a natural fluidity, almost as if it were a natural part of me. It needed to be effortlessly donned and removed, a testament to its practical design – something I could easily manage on the course. Lightweight and user-friendly were paramount, ensuring that the technology never overshadowed the pure joy and rhythm of the game itself. It had to enhance, not hinder, the experience.

What emerged from countless hours of trial and error, working with various materials and designs, was a uniquely sculpted extension, meticulously designed to integrate with my hand. This wasn't merely a strap or a simple brace; it was a bespoke piece of engineering, allowing me to grip the club with the precision and stability essential for a truly powerful swing. The moment it worked, the very first time I felt that satisfying thud of connection between club and ball, feeling the power transfer through my body, was nothing short of a eureka moment. It was a physical manifestation of a mental breakthrough.

The ability to enjoy golf, to finally experience the frustration and elation of the game on equal footing with others, was exhilarating. There was a perverse joy in shanking a shot into the rough or three-putting a green, knowing that these "mistakes and bad shots" were a universal experience, shared by every golfer, regardless of how many hands they swung with. The thrill wasn't just in hitting a good shot; it was in participating fully, in being just another person on the course, battling the course and themselves, embracing the shared human experience of the game.

My love for the game deepened with every round, every challenge, and every small victory. It became such an integral part of my life that I made a life-altering decision: I moved my family into a golf community, ensuring daily access to a course right outside our door. This wasn't just about convenience; it was about immersion, about embracing a lifestyle where the next swing was always within reach, reinforcing the gift of adaptability and problem-solving that golf brought out in me.

Can you possibly imagine what life would be like if every new endeavor, every attempt to try something new, was met with a seemingly insurmountable series of hurdles? The thought is, quite frankly, crazy, isn't it? Yet, for me, this was often the reality. The creation of that golf device wasn't just about playing a sport; it was about breaking down barriers, proving that adaptability and innovation could unlock worlds previously deemed inaccessible. It was about finding my own unique way to participate, to excel, and most importantly, to fully live.

Riding a Motorcycle

Riding a motorcycle presented a unique set of challenges for me, primarily due to the inherent difficulty of engaging the clutch with my left hand. For anyone wanting to experience the thrill of a motorcycle, a fully functioning left hand is typically a prerequisite for managing the clutch and gear shifting smoothly. This fundamental hurdle, a literal physical barrier, led me on a quest to find a way to ride despite my limitation. The desire for that sense of open-road freedom was too strong to ignore.

My journey began with a rather unconventional discovery: a 1976 Honda CB 750. This wasn't just any vintage bike; it was an automatic, a rarity even in its time, which meant it didn't have a traditional clutch. I stumbled upon it through a Penny Saver ad, a true testament to finding opportunity in unexpected places – sometimes the answer isn't what you expect. After acquiring it, I invested time and effort in its restoration, not merely for aesthetic appeal, but to ensure it was mechanically sound enough for me to assess if riding was even a possibility for me. This initial foray proved successful, confirming that I could indeed navigate and enjoy a motorcycle. This realization, this taste of freedom, ignited a new determination within me: to obtain my motorcycle license and truly embrace the open road.

With the license secured, my ambition shifted dramatically to owning a "real" bike, a true Harley-Davidson, a symbol of American freedom and power. My sights were set on a 2000 Harley Davidson Road King, a behemoth of a machine, powerful and imposing. It was a significant leap, going straight for the "big boy" without even truly knowing how to ride such a powerful bike, fueled by pure optimism. In a moment of pure optimism, I asked the salesperson if it was a good bike and, perhaps more importantly, if he would test drive it for me. To his credit, the salesperson was gracious and obliged, his willingness to oblige serving as an immediate validation of the bike's quality in my eyes – after all, we always trust the salesperson!

My next critical step led me to the service manager at the Harley Davidson dealership in Irvine, California. I presented him with my dilemma, explaining my physical limitation and my deep desire to ride a full-sized Harley. I wasn't asking for pity, but for ingenuity. Days later, he returned with a solution that was both ingenious and surprisingly simple, a true testament to creative problem-solving. He engineered the clutch to be operated by my right foot, positioning it on the floor next to the brake pedal. To complement this, he fashioned a "suicide shifter" on the tank, a classic, visually striking modification that allowed me to engage the clutch with my right foot and shift gears with my left hand by simply pushing or pulling the lever. Remarkably, he accomplished this using only stock Harley Davidson parts, a testament to his skill and ingenuity, proving that solutions can often be found with existing resources if you look creatively.

This custom modification completely transformed my riding experience. With the clutch now on the floor and the shifter on the tank, I was finally able to ride the motorcycle every day, fully engaging in the freedom and exhilaration that others had always enjoyed. This Harley, a powerful symbol of overcoming adversity and embracing the open road, remains with me to this day, a cherished testament to a creative solution, unwavering determination, and the deep satisfaction of turning a "can't" into a "can."

Flying an Airplane
From Unforeseen Skies to Custom Cockpits

I never imagined a passion for flying would ignite within me. Growing up, aviation wasn't even a distant thought. Our family's financial circumstances simply didn't allow for such aspirations, making it feel like an entirely different world. While my brother, a Naval Academy graduate, pursued flying opportunities during Desert Storm and developed a deep love for aviation, I remained largely unacquainted with its allure, my own path seemingly grounded.

Fast forward to my 33rd year. A family cruise was planned, but unforeseen business commitments forced me to cancel my personal attendance. Suddenly, I found myself with a few unexpected days of solitude and nothing but time. Wandering aimlessly into a local airport, more out of curiosity than intention, a test flight caught my eye. The instructor, perhaps sensing my burgeoning curiosity, offered me the chance to take the controls. The experience was unconventional, to say the least. Seated in the right seat of a Cessna, I found myself grappling with controls designed for a left-handed pilot, a stark contrast to my natural right-handed dominance. It was an awkward, almost comical attempt at flight, with my brain trying to re-wire years of physical habit, yet a profound spark of intrigue had been lit. The sheer novelty of being airborne, even clumsily, was captivating.

I immediately inquired about aircraft with alternative throttle configurations, seeking a design that would naturally accommodate my unique physical setup. The instructor, sensing my burgeoning interest, introduced me to the Piper Archer. Eureka! The Archer's design allowed me to grasp the yoke with my dominant right hand, while my left, without needing any complex modifications, could effortlessly manage the throttle – a simple push and pull mechanism perfectly suited to my hand. A solution had presented itself, a clear path forward, and within three intensely focused months, I proudly held my pilot's license. The ink on the license was barely dry before I knew I had to acquire my own aircraft; the freedom of the skies had become an undeniable calling.

To make the airplane truly mine, a bespoke extension of my own capabilities, I embraced the challenge of flying exclusively from the right seat. This was perfectly legal; the FAA has no mandate requiring flight from the left. I invested a significant sum to have the entire avionics suite relocated from the pilot's side to the co-pilot's, transforming the aircraft into a bespoke extension of my flying style, a cockpit perfectly tailored to my strengths. For a decade, I commanded that airplane from the right seat, a testament to my adaptability, unwavering commitment, and the power of designing systems around individual strengths rather than trying to force a fit.

Many years later, my love for flying deepened even further, urging me to explore new horizons and different aircraft. I commissioned the creation of a sophisticated custom device, a meticulously crafted attachment for the yoke on my left side. This ingenious piece of engineering enabled me to transition to a new aircraft and finally experience the standard left-seat configuration, a long-held aspiration now realized. Whether pursuing my lifelong passion for aviation from the standard left seat of an airplane or the exhilarating descent down a snowy mountain on skis, my journey has consistently demanded more than standard equipment. Each piece of custom-fabricated gear stands as a testament to a relentless pursuit of adaptation, a personal anthem to overcoming perceived limitations and embracing the extraordinary through ingenuity and persistence.

CHAPTER IV: O is for Ownership (Your Gifts) Unearthing Your Innate Gifts

Playing a Guitar

This was something I didn't have to invent a complex device for. Hallelujah! Finally, something was going my way without needing an external contraption. Instead, I simply had to learn how to treat my brain—and, more importantly, teach my brain—how to become ambidextrous in a very specific way. That's right: I had to figure out how to strum a guitar with my left hand, even though I was naturally right-handed, and finger chords with my right hand. It's akin to literally trying to take a right-handed person and force them to write perfect grammar with their left hand, then do intricate math with the right. It sounds absolutely beyond crazy to think that someone can do this, and truthfully, it took me decades of patient, persistent practice, countless hours of awkward fumbling before anything resembled music.

But the matter of fact is, I've figured it out. And no matter what seemingly insurmountable challenge you're dealing with in your life, you, too, will figure it out. You just have to stand true to the undeniable fact that you possess the ultimate choice. You must, above all else, give up the right to fail. This isn't about blind optimism or naive belief that everything will be easy; it's about cultivating an unwavering belief in your own innate capacity for adaptation, growth, and eventual triumph. It's about understanding that every setback is merely a detour, a temporary curve in the road, not a dead end, and that within you lies an untapped reservoir of resilience, creativity, and sheer determination waiting to be discovered and activated.

As I've shared in countless speeches, often with a blend of humor and poignant reflection, I personally invested over $200,000 out of my own pocket in creating these "crutches." This wasn't a casual expenditure; it was a significant financial commitment, a testament to the depth of my belief in these external aids. At the time, both society's collective wisdom and, crucially, my own deeply ingrained convictions, unequivocally believed these external aids were not just helpful but utterly indispensable for me to participate in life the way others did. Each device, every meticulously crafted contraption, was viewed as a triumph of problem-solving, born directly out of a pressing necessity and a forced innovation that pushed the boundaries of assistive technology.

Yet, in the clarifying light of hindsight, the perspective of years and experience, I can now see them for what they truly were: merely Band-Aids. They were external solutions, diligently and ingeniously applied, but ultimately superficial remedies for an internal perception of inadequacy that festered beneath the surface. It was akin to meticulously applying layer after layer of duct tape to a leaky faucet, diligently sealing every visible drip, utterly unaware that an entire toolbox, replete with the precise wrenches, washers, and pipes I truly needed for a fundamental, lasting repair, was already at my disposal, just waiting to be recognized and utilized. The real solution lay not in more external fixes, in accumulating more "things," but in a profound shift of internal perception, a powerful realization that the power to thrive resided within, not in the prosthetics and devices I so earnestly pursued.

What initially manifested as a "limitation" served as the fertile ground from which truly invaluable gifts blossomed: profound adaptability, inventive problem-solving, and an unwavering, deep-seated determination. My physical difference wasn't merely a hurdle to be overcome; it was the very soil from which these critical qualities grew and flourished, becoming integral parts of who I am. I didn't need to acquire something external to myself; I needed to unearth and wholeheartedly trust what was already present within me, waiting to be activated. This, precisely, is the essence of what I convey when I declare, "God already gave what you need to do what He wants to do." The equipment, the inherent capabilities, the unique strengths—they are already yours. They are simply waiting for you to discover, embrace, and leverage them to their fullest potential.

Echoes from Other Islands: Gifts Born from Adversity

This powerful pattern of adversity forging extraordinary gifts is not unique to my story, or to anyone's, really. It's a universal truth. Countless public figures and everyday heroes have walked similar paths, their perceived limitations becoming the crucible for their greatest strengths, showcasing how challenges can be catalysts.

- **Helen Keller:** Blind and deaf from a very young age, her immense challenges didn't crush her spirit. Instead, they led to the development of profound gifts in communication, unwavering advocacy for others with disabilities, and an indomitable spirit that inspired millions. She didn't just overcome; she used her unique perspective, born from profound adversity, to literally change the world for others, showing us all what's truly possible when you tap into inner strength. As she famously said, "I am only one, but still I am one. I cannot do everything, but still I can do something; and because I cannot do everything, I will not refuse to do the something that I can do." Talk about owning your gifts!
- **Stephen Hawking:** Diagnosed with ALS at a young age and confined to a wheelchair, eventually unable to speak without assistance, he possessed an unparalleled intellectual gift. His physical limitations did not diminish his capacity to expand our understanding of the universe. In fact, they arguably intensified his internal focus. His resilience, his profound curiosity, and his unwavering focus were gifts honed by his circumstances; his mind soared even as his body struggled,

pushing the boundaries of scientific thought.
- **Jim Abbott:** Born without a right hand, he defied all conventional expectations by becoming a successful Major League Baseball pitcher. His gift isn't just incredible athletic ability, but the profound innovation and relentless dedication required to develop a unique pitching style that allowed him to compete at the highest level of professional sports. He literally found a new way to play the game, demonstrating that boundaries are often just challenges for ingenuity.
- **Victoria Arlen:** After a rare autoimmune disorder left her unable to walk, speak, or move her arms, she not only recovered against all odds but harnessed gifts of fierce resilience, unwavering determination, and an unbreakable spirit to become a Paralympic gold medalist and a vibrant television personality. Her journey is a powerful testament to turning profound adversity into a launchpad for extraordinary achievement and widespread inspiration.

These individuals, and countless more like them, didn't let their "islands" of difference or difficulty define them in a limiting way. Instead, those very circumstances, those challenging terrains, actually helped to unearth or sculpt the unique gifts they used to achieve extraordinary things and inspire millions. Their stories echo the profound truth: your challenges are often the very birthplace of your greatest strengths. What feels like a burden, a heavy weight you've carried, might just be your unique superpower in disguise, waiting for you to recognize it and put it to work.

Actionable Strategies: Unearthing Your Own Treasures

THE ISLAND STRATEGIES

Recognizing and utilizing your innate gifts is not a passive process, my friend. It requires conscious effort, deep introspection, and a willingness to see yourself in a beautiful new light.

Here are some actionable strategies to help you gently excavate the hidden treasures on your island:

- **The Adversity Audit: Mining Challenges for Strengths**
  - **Exercise:** Take some quiet time to reflect on the most significant challenges or difficulties you've faced in your life. For each challenge:

    - What specific actions did you take to get through it? Did you fight, adapt, seek help, or simply endure?
    - What internal resources (e.g., determination, patience, creativity, courage, empathy, problem-solving skills) did you have to call upon to navigate it? What did you discover you had inside you that you perhaps didn't realize before?
    - What did you learn about yourself during and after this difficult period? What did it teach you about your own resilience, your capacity for growth, or your inner strength?
    - What new skills or perspectives did you develop as a direct result of going through it? Did it force you to think differently, to innovate, or to learn something entirely new about yourself or the world?

Often, the very qualities that saw you through your toughest times are your most profound, yet often unacknowledged, gifts. Resilience, for example, isn't something you're just born with at full strength; it's a gift cultivated and hardened through overcoming. My father, who served 49 years in the Army, taught me a powerful lesson that resonates here: "When you go into battle, you go in there with brothers and sisters in arms. But you don't leave them there." This philosophy extends to our own internal battles and how we cultivate the strength to fight for our dreams. You don't leave yourself behind; you bring all of your past, even the hard parts, along as fuel for your future journey.

- **The Passion & Purpose Detector: Following Your Energy**
  - **Exercise:** Answer these questions from the heart, as I often ask in my seminars, letting your intuition guide you:

    - "What makes you sing?" (What brings you genuine, unadulterated joy? What activities make you lose track of time, making hours feel like minutes?)
    - "What makes you dream?" (What possibilities truly excite you and ignite your imagination? What future do you find yourself constantly envisioning and yearning for?)
    - "What makes you cry?" (What injustices, or moments of profound connection or breathtaking beauty, move you deeply? What stirs your soul to its very core, perhaps with sadness, empathy, or awe?)

CHAPTER IV: O is for Ownership (Your Gifts) Unearthing Your Innate Gifts

The answers to these questions are incredibly illuminating; they point directly towards your core values and deepest passions. The activities and pursuits that make you feel most alive, most engaged, and most authentically you are often deeply connected to your innate gifts. When you're operating from these gifts, tasks feel less like burdensome work and more like a natural, joyful expression of who you are. It's like finally finding your true calling, where effort feels effortless because you're tapping into your natural flow.

- **Reframing Perceived Weaknesses into Unique Assets**
  o The Alchemist's Touch: Many of us carry around aspects of ourselves that we, or perhaps others, have labeled as weaknesses. It's time to gently, but firmly, challenge those limiting labels.
  o **Exercise:**
    - List 3-5 things you genuinely consider to be your weaknesses or areas where you often feel "less than." Be completely honest with yourself here; this is for your eyes only.
    - For each item, ask yourself: "In what context, or from what perspective, could this perceived weakness actually be a hidden strength or a unique asset?"

    For example: If you've been told you're "too sensitive," could your true gift be profound empathy, deep intuition, and an ability to connect with others on a visceral level? If you've been called "stubborn," might your treasure be unwavering tenacity, incredible resolve, and an unshakeable commitment to your goals? Are you "too quiet"? Perhaps your gift is deep observation, thoughtful analysis, and the ability to listen with profound presence before speaking. My "one hand" was, for many years, perceived by others and sometimes by myself as a significant weakness, a severe limitation. But, as you've read, it became the powerful catalyst for intense innovation, extraordinary problem-solving skills, and a unique perspective on overcoming adversity. Your perceived flaws might just be your greatest gifts in disguise, waiting patiently for you to bravely reframe them. It's truly all about how you choose to look at it, and the meaning you decide to assign.

- **Leveraging Your Innate Gifts to Navigate Challenges**
    - **Activation is Key:** Once you begin to identify and courageously reframe your gifts, the next crucial step is to consciously leverage them. You don't just find the treasure; you use it!

    - **Strategy:** When facing a new challenge or making an important decision:
        - **Pause for a moment and ask**: "Which of my innate gifts are best suited to help me navigate this particular situation?"
        - How can you approach the problem in a way that genuinely plays to your strengths, rather than focusing on or highlighting areas where you feel less capable or confident?

            For example, if you've identified "creativity" as a core gift, how can you apply imaginative, out-of-the-box thinking to a seemingly intractable problem that others are struggling with? If "resilience" is a profound core gift, how can you consciously draw on your past experiences of overcoming adversity to fuel your current efforts and maintain momentum? Living deliberately means consciously choosing to engage your strengths in every aspect of your life. It's about aligning your actions with your innate capabilities, which not only leads to better outcomes but also to a deeper, more profound sense of authenticity and personal fulfillment. You'll feel more authentically you when you're consciously using your natural talents.

The Divine Endowment: "God Already Gave What You Need"

I want to circle back to that foundational belief, a truth that has guided me through so much: "God already gave what you need to do what He wants to do." This isn't just a comforting phrase, a pleasant thought; it's a profound, liberating truth about your inherent design, your very blueprint. Your gifts—whether they are obvious talents that shine brightly or the quieter, deeper strengths forged in the crucible of adversity—are not accidental. They are part of your essential toolkit, divinely endowed or inherently present within you, perfectly designed to equip you for your unique journey on your "Island of One."

The process of unearthing these gifts is not about acquiring something new from the outside, something you lack. It's an internal excavation, a gentle archeological dig within your own being. It's about peeling back the layers of self-doubt, the subtle influences of societal conditioning, and the fears that may have obscured what has been within you all along, waiting to be rediscovered. As I intimately discovered through my own journey, I didn't need more prosthetics or external devices to live fully and vibrantly; I needed to tap into the boundless ingenuity, the tenacious determination, and the creative problem-solving abilities that were already an undeniable part of my being. As Lao Tzu famously said, "When you realize there is nothing lacking, the whole world belongs to you." You already have everything you need to start, to build, to thrive.

Your Gifts: The First Key to Thriving

Unearthing and wholeheartedly embracing your innate gifts is the first, crucial key to unlocking unstoppable resilience and truly thriving on your island. These gifts are your unique advantages, your personal superpowers. They are the internal resources that will help you overcome obstacles, create a life of profound purpose and meaning, and navigate your path with courage, grace, and undeniable authenticity. The journey of self-discovery is ongoing, a beautiful unfolding. Be patient with yourself. Be curious. And most importantly, deeply and truly believe in the incredible treasures that lie within you. You don't need to look outside for what you need to succeed; you need to look within and activate the incredible gifts you already possess. This is your birthright, your unique blueprint for a life not just survived, but truly thrived, in every beautiful sense of the word.

CHAPTER V: M is for Manage (Your Time) Mastering Your Time

CHAPTER V
M is for Manage *(Your Time)*
Mastering Your Time

"The critical difference, the factor that separates a life of meaningful accomplishment from one of regret, lies not in the amount of time received, but in how that time is invested."

Mastering Your Time: The Currency of Your Island

Let's dive into something we all juggle every single day, something that feels incredibly precious and sometimes, well, a little overwhelming: time. This chapter is about the 'M' in The C.O.M.P.A.S.S. System: **Manage**! It's all about learning how to truly master your time... or at least, how to stop letting it master *you*. And this whole idea really starts with figuring out "the ONE thing." What's that one thing in your life that, if you tweaked it, would just dramatically shift everything else?

My dad, who spent an incredible 49 years in the Army, taught me

CHAPTER V: M is for Manage (Your Time) Mastering Your Time

his "one thing," and honestly, it completely revolutionized how I managed my time and ran my companies: "Never touch a paper twice." It sounds simple, right? But it wasn't about literal paper. It was about efficiency, about making a decision *now*. If you pick up an email, respond to it now. If the phone rings, handle it now or let it go to voicemail. No deferring tasks. This simple rule became my core principle for focused action, cutting right through procrastination and allowing me to manage so many different ventures all at once. To really keep that thought with me every day, I even carry a small wooden "round-to-it" chip in my pocket – it's a silly little thing, but it's a tangible reminder that there's always a way to "get around to it" right *now*, instead of pushing it off. And you know what? It works!

If we think of your unique Gifts as the hidden treasures buried within your island's soil, then Time? Time is truly your island's most precious, non-renewable resource. It's the very currency you use to buy your experiences, to build your dreams, and to live out your purpose. Every single person on this planet, from the wealthiest to the humblest, has the exact same 24 hours in a day. The real, critical difference – the thing that truly separates a life of meaningful accomplishment from one of regret – isn't about how much time you *get*, but about how you *invest* that time.

You've been given one precious, finite opportunity to experience and shape your life. So, as I've often emphasized, it's absolutely imperative that you make it count. Too many of us just kind of drift through our days, allowing circumstances and external demands to dictate our actions. We become reactors instead of deliberate creators, existing but not truly living. But here's the good news: this can totally change. The moment you decide to master your time, you begin to reclaim the captaincy of your life. This mastery, though, starts with identifying and then, gently but firmly, vanquishing the little thieves that are constantly trying to steal this irreplaceable currency from you. After all, time flies whether you're having fun or frantically trying to catch up!

As William Penn wisely noted, "Time is what we want most, but what we use worst." Let's change that for you.

Identifying and Conquering the Thieves of Your Hours

There are these sneaky forces always at work, just eager to steal your precious moments, leaving you feeling depleted and unproductive. These are the "Time Robbers," and simply understanding them is the first big step to disarming them.

- **Worry: The Thief of the Present**
  Worry is like a phantom that haunts your present by painting these terrifying, yet often baseless, pictures of the future. It's that gnawing anxiety that can jolt you awake at 2 a.m., your mind racing with "what ifs" and worst-case scenarios. We often, almost unconsciously, grant ourselves the "right" to worry, sometimes mistaking it for being diligent or truly concerned. But, as I've asked before, echoing a timeless wisdom, "who of you, by worrying, can add a single hour to their life?" Worry is a profound noise in our lives. It's our misguided attempt to control an uncontrollable future by implementing our assumptions of what might happen. The result? A paralyzed present, where precious time is just consumed by fear rather than productive action. I know this intimately. When my first daughter, Kayla, was born, my wife and I just sat there, staring at her in the crib, almost afraid to go to sleep. One of us stayed up all night, just watching her, making sure she was breathing. That was worry stealing precious rest and peace, rooted deep in my own childhood fears of being born with a physical difference, projecting those anxieties onto her. It was exhausting and utterly

unproductive.

- **Want: The Siren Call of Instant Gratification**
The second great time robber is "Want"—that relentless craving for instant gratification, often fueled by the world around us. We're subtly conditioned to believe that true peace or happiness can be purchased, whether it's through an impulse buy online or the fleeting satisfaction of a new possession. When boredom, anger, or sadness strikes, how often do we turn to "retail therapy" or mindless scrolling for a quick fix? This constant seeking of external solutions and temporary pleasures is a huge distraction. It's another layer of noise that pulls us away from investing our time in what truly nourishes our spirit and genuinely moves us toward our goals. The ability to delay instant gratification, as I've learned and often share, is a cornerstone of any significant success. Who knew self-control could be so... un-fun in the moment? I confess, I'm absolutely guilty sometimes.

I once bought a pair of Louis Vuitton shoes for $1,000. Why? Because I "wanted" to feel a certain way, to fulfill a superficial desire, not a true, deep need. I was chasing a fleeting sense of elevated status, a quiet whisper of acceptance, or perhaps a temporary boost to my self-esteem that I mistakenly believed could be purchased. It was a momentary indulgence, a quick rush, much like a sugar high that hits hard and then inevitably crashes. The initial thrill of owning something so outwardly luxurious, of feeling momentarily "better" or more "important," quickly evaporated. It was a fleeting high that dissolved into the everyday, leaving me not with lasting fulfillment, but simply lighter pockets and no real inner change. In fact, that brief external validation often highlighted the very internal void I was trying to fill, making the original feeling of lack even more apparent once the novelty wore off. It was a stark reminder that true contentment doesn't come in a designer box; it comes from within, from genuinely addressing what our hearts and souls truly need, not just what our egos momentarily crave.

- **Procrastination: The Comfortable Cage**
  Perhaps the most pervasive time robber of all is Procrastination. It's truly an art, isn't it? The art of putting things off, allowing unresolved tasks and unmade decisions to pile up like mental clutter. Why do we procrastinate? Sometimes it's that perfectionism peeking through – the fear that if we can't do it perfectly, we shouldn't do it at all. Other times, a task just seems so overwhelmingly large that we simply don't even begin. We might tell ourselves, "I'd rather watch Netflix than do something else." This is the lure of escape. We come home, seeking refuge from the day's pressures, and fall into the easy routine of binge-watching, anything to avoid facing the challenges or tasks that await us. *"Man, we spend more time as human beings escaping life than living life,"* I've often observed. Procrastination keeps you locked in familiar patterns, even if those patterns are unproductive and unfulfilling. It's like endlessly organizing your sock drawer when you have a mountain of laundry waiting!

My father, an Army veteran of 49 years, instilled a profoundly simple yet powerful rule: "Never touch a paper twice." In his world, every document demanded immediate, decisive action – no deferring. This wasn't just about efficiency; it was about the clarity and commitment vital in a military context, preventing backlog. For our modern lives,

CHAPTER V: M is for Manage (Your Time) Mastering Your Time

this wisdom translates directly to emails, messages, and tasks. The essence is: if you engage with it, complete it, delegate it, or discard it *immediately*. Don't let it linger, demanding mental bandwidth later. This singular focus became my personal "one thing" to dismantle procrastination, fundamentally transforming how I managed my diverse companies. It cleared mental clutter, accelerated decision-making, and fostered a proactive workflow that truly made a difference. To reinforce this daily, I carry a small wooden "round-to-it" chip – a tangible, constant nudge to act *now*. This simple token is a powerful symbol, consistently breaking the inertia of procrastination and freeing up precious mental space, ensuring tasks are handled with swift, focused intention rather than deferred into a growing pile of stress that often never gets addressed.

- **External Distractions: The Constant Barrage of Noise**
  Beyond our internal struggles with worry, want, and procrastination, we are just constantly bombarded by external distractions. The television blares, sometimes just as background noise. Our phones buzz incessantly with notifications. We feel this almost irresistible compulsion to be "chatterboxes," whether in person, on calls, or through texts. This constant need for external stimuli, this aversion to silence, creates an environment where focused action becomes nearly impossible. As the "Noise Level Test" I often use reveals, many of us live in a state of "jittery chaos," our lives too loud and too busy to hear our own inner guidance or to truly concentrate on what matters most. It's a miracle we get anything done, really. It's like trying to have a deep conversation in the middle of a rock concert!

Actionable Strategies: Forging a Life of Intention

Mastering your time isn't about finding more hours in the day, is it? It's about making the hours you *do* have truly count. This requires intentionality, some smart planning, and a genuine commitment to focused action. As Michael Altshuler cleverly put it, "The bad news is time flies. The good news is you're the pilot." So, let's get you in the cockpit!

Practical Ways to Live with Intention: Setting Goals, Prioritizing, and Focusing

- **Set Clear Goals:** You simply can't hit a target you can't see, right? Before you can manage your time effectively, you absolutely have to know what you're aiming for. This means translating your dreams and desires—those things that make you sing, dream, and cry—into concrete, actionable goals. What do you *really* want to achieve? What kind of life do you want to build on your island? Write it down. Make it specific.
- **Prioritize Ruthlessly:** Not all tasks are created equal. Identify the activities that will move you closest to your goals and give them top priority. This often means learning to say "no"—no to distractions, no to commitments that don't truly align with your purpose, no to requests that drain your energy without adding significant value. Saying "yes" to your most important priorities often requires saying a firm "no" to other things. Sometimes, "no" is a complete sentence. And a very powerful one.
- **Embrace Focused Action (Single-Tasking):** The myth of multitasking is a dangerous one. True productivity comes from focused, dedicated effort on one task at a time. When

CHAPTER V: M is for Manage (Your Time) Mastering Your Time

you're working on something, give it your undivided attention. Close other tabs, silence notifications, and just immerse yourself in the task at hand. Your brain will absolutely thank you. It's like having a laser pointer for your attention instead of a broad floodlight.

- **Schedule Your Days:** Treat your time like the precious commodity it is. Plan your days. I schedule everything: work blocks, meetings, exercise, meals, even "dead time" for thinking or journaling. A schedule transforms intention into action. Don't just allow your day to happen to you; truly *design* it.
- **Get Sufficient Rest:** A tired mind is, plain and simple, an unproductive mind. Prioritize 7-8 hours of quality sleep. This is non-negotiable for peak performance. Think of it as charging your personal battery. You wouldn't expect your phone to run on empty, would you?
- **Rise Early:** Many incredibly successful individuals harness the quiet, uninterrupted hours of the early morning to focus on their most important work or personal development before the world's demands begin. The early bird catches the worm, and probably finishes their to-do list before noon! It's truly a secret weapon for deep focus.
- **Utilize "Dead Time":** Those moments spent waiting in line, commuting, or between appointments can be reclaimed. Use this time for reading, listening to educational podcasts, jotting down ideas, or planning. Always be thinking (ABT). Make every minute count.
- **Make Time for Yourself:** Deliberately schedule time for activities that truly rejuvenate you and connect you with yourself, whether it's exercise, meditation, hobbies, or simply quiet reflection. Yes, even introverts need to schedule their solitude! It's not selfish; it's absolutely essential for your well-being.

Eliminating the "Noise" to Hear Your Own Inner Guidance

Our modern world is incredibly noisy, isn't it? To truly hear the quiet voice of your own inner guidance, your intuition, you must consciously create pockets of silence.

- **Turn Off the Noise Machines:** The first step for many is to simply turn off the television. It's often what I call a "revenue degeneration machine," consuming hours that could be spent on far more fulfilling or productive activities. Be mindful of how much time you spend on social media, aimlessly surfing the internet, or even with constant music if it prevents focused thought. Sometimes, the best channel is just "off."
- **Practice Stillness:** Whether you call it meditation, prayer, or simply "time with yourself," regularly disconnect from the external chaos and connect with your internal world. As I've often said, "You've got to go inside of you... because whatever's inside of you is going to come out." It's in these moments of quiet contemplation that clarity often emerges, and you can truly hear your own thoughts.
- **Listen to Yourself:** The answers you seek are often already within you. By reducing external noise, you create the space to hear your own thoughts, feel your own emotions, and discern your own truth. Your inner guidance is your most reliable compass, but it needs a quiet space to speak.

Making Each Day Count: "What Will You Do With the Time You Have Left?"

Remember the eulogy exercise we talked about? The purpose wasn't to be morbid, but to bring a really sharp focus to the finite nature of your time. If you knew your days were numbered, how would you spend them? The truth is, they *are* numbered. Every

CHAPTER V: M is for Manage (Your Time) Mastering Your Time

day that passes is one less day you have to make your mark, to live your purpose, to experience joy.

"You don't have much time," I often tell people. "Many people act as if they have an infinite amount of time. We do not." This realization shouldn't be a source of panic, but a powerful catalyst for deliberate action. Start doing what you truly want to do before it's too late. I learned this the hard way, working 18 hours a day to get my family back on top during tough financial times. It wasn't just about money; it was about making every single hour count to secure their future and our family's well-being, to pull us out of a very dark place. Every minute became a strategic investment.

The mastery of time is really the mastery of life itself. Your success or failure, your fulfillment or regret, will ultimately be determined by how you choose to invest this irreplaceable currency. So, let's stop allowing your days to be stolen by worry, by wanting things that don't truly serve you, by procrastination, and by endless distractions. Reclaim your hours. Live deliberately. Make each day, each moment, truly count. The power to transform your life is embedded in the choices you make about your time, starting right now. It's time to stop hitting snooze on your life.

CHAPTER VI
P is for Perspective *(Your Past)*
Transforming Anchors into Launchpads

"Your fear is just an illusion showing you an assumed future based on an uncomfortable past."

Reclaiming Your Past

You know, there's this incredible power in how we look at things, especially when it comes to our past. This chapter is all about that, the 'P' in The C.O.M.P.A.S.S. System: Perspective! It's about learning to transform your past… because honestly, who wants to carry all that old emotional baggage around forever? Seriously, imagine trying to sail your beautiful island with a giant, heavy anchor dragging behind you!

For so many of us, the past can feel exactly like that – a weighty anchor, tying us down to old hurts, those sneaky limiting beliefs, and patterns of behavior that just stop us from sailing towards the amazing future we dream about. But what if I told you that this very anchor could actually be reforged into a launchpad? What if those experiences you believe define you in negative ways actually hold the keys to your greatest strengths?

The time has come to start gently reclaiming your past. It's about understanding just how much it has influenced you, not so you can stay shackled by it, but so you can truly harness its lessons, transform any lingering pain, and use it as a powerful boost for the incredible life you're meant to live. As Mary Pickford so wisely observed, "The past cannot be changed. The future is yet in your power." Your past is done, wrapped up, but your future? That's still very much in your hands.

Your Past: Just Data, Not Your Destiny

One of the most persistent myths we tend to live by is that our past somehow dictates our future. It's like we carry yesterday's weather into today's forecast, automatically expecting the same storms just because we've weathered them before. As I've often said, so many of us "believe things you assume to be true that really are just assumptions you created from your past experiences." We make decisions today not based on objective truth, but on "how I experienced it, not the truth. They're not always the same." This is exactly how the past can become a kind of self-fulfilling prophecy, and we unknowingly become prisoners of our own biased memories.

Think about the story of Henry Molaison, the man who, after brain surgery, couldn't form new memories. In a devastating way, he was truly stuck in his past, unable to build a new future from fresh experiences. While his case was extreme, many of us live a less literal version of this. We constantly replay "old tapes" in our minds – those persistent mental loops of past failures, criticisms, or even traumas. These aren't just fleeting thoughts; they're

CHAPTER VI: P is for Perspective (Your Past)

deeply grooved neural pathways, our brain's well-meaning but misguided attempt to "protect" us by constantly rehashing what went wrong or what might go wrong. This constant re-engagement effectively freezes us in time, stopping us from writing new narratives for our lives and preventing us from truly embracing the opportunities that lie in our future. It's like being caught in a psychological Groundhog Day, reliving the same emotional low points over and over, all while the vibrant, unpredictable present slips through our fingers. The consequence? Missed opportunities, less spontaneity, self-sabotage, and a deep emotional exhaustion that makes stepping into the unknown feel like trying to climb Mount Everest in flip-flops.

Growing up near Checkpoint Charlie in West Berlin, witnessing that stark division and the desperate desire for freedom, left an indelible mark on me. I can still recall the scene so vividly: my family – Mom, Dad, my three brothers and sisters, all of us crammed into our 1977 VW Bus. The air itself felt thick with the weight of separation, the constant vigilance, the silent longing etched on the faces of those on both sides of that brutal divide. My dad, in his uniform, was showing our passports, the tension palpable in the small space of the bus. Just before we were waved through, we heard a chilling story that instantly quieted all of us. A person, caught in the middle of Checkpoint Charlie, had been killed when they tried to turn their car around. That knowledge, right there, just before our own passage, could have easily left me with a pervasive sense of fear or cynicism. This environment could have taught me to see the world as inherently dangerous, opportunities as scarce, and freedom as an elusive dream. Instead, those powerful memories, especially that stark warning, became valuable data points about human resilience, the incredible importance of choice, and that deep-seated urge to overcome limitations. It wasn't passive observation; it was an active interpretation that sought to understand the universal human drive to break free from self-imposed or external constraints, transforming a chilling historical reality into a personal fuel for navigating my own 'walls' and embracing radical responsibility. It showed me that even in the most restricted environments, the human spirit yearns for and can find freedom.

So, the very first step in reclaiming your past is to gently, but firmly, challenge the idea that it has some unbreakable hold on you. Your history is absolutely a part of your story, but it does not have to be the only story you tell, nor does it have to be the concluding chapter. You get to write the next one.

How Memories and "Significant Emotional Events" Shape Your Present

Our past really does imprint itself upon us, not like a light sketch that's easily erased, but often like a deep engraving. This happens primarily through the power of our memories and what sociologist Morris Massey so aptly termed "Significant Emotional Events" (SEEs). As we've touched upon, these SEEs aren't necessarily singular, earth-shattering catastrophes, though they certainly can be. They encompass a wide spectrum of experiences – moments of intense, unbridled joy that set a standard for happiness, profound and disorienting loss that truly reshapes our understanding of the world, sharp, searing humiliation that chips away at our self-worth, or exhilarating, triumphant achievement that briefly makes us feel invincible. Each of these events, heavy with emotional charge, carves deep channels into our psyche. They become powerful, often subconscious, reference points, like the navigational stars by which we unknowingly steer our present choices, our gut reactions, and especially, the fears that whisper limitations to us in the quiet of the night. These imprints are so powerful because the human brain is wired to remember emotionally charged events more vividly; it's a survival mechanism, but one that can also keep us tethered to outdated responses, like a ship continually returning to a stormy port.

That "one-handed-monkey" taunt on the kickball field wasn't just a fleeting childhood insult for me; it was a **Significant Emotional Event**. It landed with the force of a physical blow, a painful imprint that had the very real potential to set me on a path of lifelong shame, self-doubt, and withdrawal. I could have internalized that label, allowing it to become the defining characteristic of my existence. But my father, seeing my tears and anger, pulled over the school bus on the military base and defended me, proclaiming, "This is my son. This is how God made him. This is who he is. If you have a problem with that, you come see me and you bring your parents along." That moment didn't erase the pain, but it absolutely transformed it into pride and a fierce belief in myself. It became a launchpad. My father's words were like a shield, protecting me and helping me reframe that painful experience into a source of strength.

Many people carry similar imprints, perhaps less visible but no less potent: the sting of persistent childhood teasing that morphs into adult social anxiety; the dismissive words of a critical teacher that unknowingly silence a budding passion; the betrayal in a failed relationship that fosters a deep-seated mistrust of intimacy; or a significant career setback that cultivates a paralyzing fear of failure in future endeavors. I've experienced career setbacks myself, going bankrupt not once, but twice. Each time, "I felt as if I was smaller than an enigma. I had failed society's pulse." These failures could have been crippling anchors, but I consciously chose to transform them into data points, lessons learned, and fuel for building new businesses. They were painful, yes, but they taught me invaluable lessons about resilience, strategy, and getting back up, even when it feels utterly impossible. These events, and the potent cocktail of emotions tied to them—be it fear, anger, sadness, guilt, or even a distorted sense of responsibility—become the colored lenses through which we view and interpret subsequent, even vaguely similar, situations. A person consistently criticized by a parent during formative years might, as an adult, perceive constructive feedback from a boss as a personal attack, reacting with defensiveness rooted in those old wounds.

The Lobster at the Ritz-Carlton: A Birthday Celebration Gone Sideways

Let me share another pivotal moment, a "Significant Emotional Event" that, while seemingly minor on the surface, resonated deeply with my understanding of being treated "differently." It was a weekend that started with so much promise: my wife, two of my closest friends, Ron and Mark, and their significant others, all gathered in Palm Springs for a truly grand celebration—my birthday at the luxurious Ritz-Carlton. The anticipation was palpable. We arrived at the resort with simple, joyful plans: hours of relaxation by the shimmering pool, delicious meals, and the sheer pleasure of each other's company. What could be better than celebrating a birthday surrounded by your favorite people at an awesome resort?

That evening, the grand celebration moved to the resort's upscale restaurant. It was my birthday, after all, and I envisioned the most awesome meal in the world. My heart was set on a truly magnificent lobster. And wouldn't you know it, a whole lobster was proudly featured on the menu! Without hesitation, I ordered

CHAPTER VI: P is for Perspective (Your Past)

it, picturing the quintessential fine dining experience.

The shock that followed when my plate arrived was immediate and profound. Instead of the majestic, intact Maine lobster I had eagerly anticipated, there on my plate were small, perfectly diced squares of lobster meat, meticulously removed from its shell. The shell itself was conspicuously absent. "What is this?" I asked the waitress, my voice a mix of confusion and disbelief. Her reply, delivered with an air of well-meaning but utterly misplaced assurance, was, "Oh, we thought it would be better for you."

Better for *me*? The words hit me with a force that went beyond mere culinary disappointment. It was a moment of stark, bewildering realization: they had made an assumption about *my* needs, about *my* capabilities, about *me*, without ever asking. They had "helped" me in a way I neither wanted nor needed, fundamentally altering my experience based on a preconceived notion. It felt like a miniature, yet incredibly potent, symbol of every time I had been underestimated, overlooked, or treated as if I couldn't handle things for myself.

I was utterly blown away. "No," I insisted, my voice firmer now, "I want a lobster, properly, in the shell, with everything else." The restaurant staff, sensing my distress, took the plate away. What happened next only intensified my feelings: they brought the lobster back, having literally retrieved the shells from the trash to reassemble the diced meat within them, presenting a grotesque parody of what I had ordered.

At that moment, something inside me just snapped. I was losing it. The frustration, the feeling of being misunderstood, of having my wishes disregarded, and above all, the underlying sting of being treated "differently" in a way that felt condescending, was overwhelming. I got up from the table, walked away, tears welling in my eyes. The joy of my birthday celebration had evaporated, replaced by a profound sense of isolation and hurt. My friends, witnessing my distress, immediately rallied, bringing the manager into the fray. The entire evening devolved into a nightmare of perceived misjudgment and being treated without the respect I craved. I found myself sitting outside near the pool, tears streaming down my face, feeling completely exposed and alone at the magnificent Ritz-Carlton.

The manager, after my friends' vigorous complaints and strong advocacy on my behalf, eventually approached me. He genuinely asked what I wanted. Through my tears, I articulated the core of my pain: "I wanted to have a great birthday celebration without thinking that I was different."

And in a testament to the power of clear communication and genuine apology, they made amends. To compensate for the terrible experience, the resort comped everyone's entire weekend stay, arranged for a private car to take us to an exquisite restaurant in the desert, and took care of that entire bill. Yes, we went deep to the tune of over $5,000 for a party of 6. There was something special about a bottle of Louie paired with Opus and the finest of everything one could imagine. A little retail therapy went a long way. The Ritz went over and above to offer a thorough and heartfelt apologies for their "ignorance and mistake."

That experience is one I will never forget. It's a stark, visceral reminder that how you are born, how you are perceived, is indeed part of your makeup, and sometimes, others make assumptions about that makeup that can lead to deeply painful moments. This incident became a powerful "data point" for me, cementing the concept of unintended bias and the profound impact of small actions on a person's sense of belonging and worth. It

CHAPTER VI: P is for Perspective (Your Past)

underscored the importance of never assuming someone's needs or capabilities, and the ever-present reality that perceptions, even well-meaning ones, can wound. It continues to be a constant, living reality, reinforcing the lesson that we must challenge assumptions, both external and internal, about who we are and what we are capable of.

This deeply ingrained mechanism of emotional memory is precisely why, as I emphasize in the Introduction and throughout my work, "Your fear is just an illusion showing you an assumed future based on an uncomfortable past." This statement is foundational to understanding how we often become prisoners of our own history. Fear, in its most common and debilitating form, rarely springs from a clear, objective, and present danger that requires an immediate fight-or-flight response. More often, it's an echo from the caverns of our past, a shadow cast by an old pain, a learned response that was once adaptive but is now simply restrictive. Your mind, in its well-intentioned but sometimes misguided attempt to protect you from repeating past hurts, takes that old discomfort, that memory of failure or pain, and projects it onto the blank canvas of a potential future scenario. This projection creates a compelling, often terrifying, illusion of impending doom, failure, or rejection. It's as if your past experiences are operating like an outdated software program, running scripts that are no longer relevant to your current operating system or environment.

Consider the entrepreneur whose first business venture ended in a painful bankruptcy (a significant SEE). The fear they experience when contemplating a new business idea isn't solely about the inherent risks of the new venture itself; it's heavily saturated with the remembered taste of ashes from the previous failure—the financial strain, the public humiliation, the personal sense of inadequacy. That past pain becomes a powerful deterrent, an internal voice screaming, "Don't do it! Remember what happened last time?" Similarly, if a past romantic relationship ended in a devastating heartbreak due to infidelity (another potent SEE), the fear of vulnerability and commitment in a new relationship is massively amplified by the echoes of that betrayal. Every new partner is viewed through a lens of suspicion, every innocent action potentially misinterpreted, because the past imprint insists that history is doomed to repeat itself. This isn't rational; it's a conditioned emotional response, the past bleeding into and distorting the present.

The subtle and insidious ways we allow our past to dictate our present are manifold. We allow forgotten promises (perhaps promises we made to ourselves and broke, leading to a sense of unreliability), the ingrained positions of influential figures from our youth (like a parent who always said, "You'll never amount to much"), or even the collective anxieties of our peer groups to pave the way for the choices we make today, often without a flicker of conscious realization. We find ourselves "judging your present by your past," a phrase that encapsulates how we superimpose old narratives onto new realities. You might unconsciously avoid a challenging career path, not because you lack the aptitude, but because a teacher once casually remarked you weren't "cut out for" that kind of work (an SEE that became an accepted truth). You might struggle with forming deep, trusting connections because a childhood friend betrayed your confidence (an SEE that taught you, erroneously, that people are fundamentally untrustworthy). These imprints, these emotionally charged conclusions drawn from past events, become the invisible fences around your island. They define the perceived boundaries of your capabilities, your worthiness, and your potential for happiness, effectively limiting where you believe you can go, what you believe you can achieve, and who you believe you can become. These fences are not made of stone or steel, but of beliefs and fears far more difficult to dismantle because they reside within us.

Actionable Strategies: Transforming Anchors into Launchpads

Understanding how the past imprints us is crucial, but insight alone isn't enough, is it? The real goal is transformation. It's about taking those experiences that feel like anchors and, with a bit of courage and intention, turning them into the very fuel that launches you forward. After all, "We are not victims of our past; we are pioneers of our future." – Anonymous.

Techniques for Gently Reframing Painful Memories into Lessons of Strength and Resilience

Your past doesn't change, but your relationship to it absolutely can. Reframing is about changing the meaning you assign to those past events, especially the painful ones.

- **The Survivor's Narrative:** Instead of seeing yourself as a victim of past circumstances, consciously choose to reframe your story as that of a survivor. What did you endure? What did you learn from it? How did it, even in its difficulty, contribute to the amazing person you are today? My "one-handed-monkey" moment didn't make me a victim; it ignited a fury, a determination that became a defining strength. I was, as I've come to understand, "designed to overcome everything." Your challenges, too, have equipped you. You are a survivor, and that's a truly powerful identity to embrace.

- **Extract the Lesson, Release the Emotion:** Every painful experience holds a lesson, often many lessons. The challenge is to gently extract that wisdom without staying emotionally entangled in the original pain. It's a bit like learning from a bad recipe without having to eat the whole thing again. You take the knowledge, but leave the bad taste behind.
- **Journaling Exercise:** Try writing about a painful memory. First, just describe the event and the emotions you felt. Really let yourself feel them, without judgment. Then, gently shift your focus: What did you learn about yourself from this experience? What did you learn about others, or about life itself? What strengths did you discover or develop because you went through it? Could you have handled it differently with the knowledge you have now (not to bring up regret, but to really solidify your learning)?
- **Gratitude for the Growth:** This one can be challenging, I know, but try to find just a sliver of gratitude, not for the pain itself, but for the growth it may have spurred. Did the hardship make you more compassionate? More resilient? More determined? Did it clarify what you truly value? It's not about being thankful for the pain, but truly thankful for what the pain taught you.

Exercises for Understanding How Your Past Influences Your Current "Island" Experience

To truly change how your past influences you, you first need to become really aware of how it's showing up in your present.

- **Pattern Recognition:**
  - **Reflection Questions:** Are there any recurring negative patterns in your life (maybe in relationships, career choices, or even financial habits)?
  - When these patterns pop up, what past experiences or feelings do they remind you of?

- What beliefs about yourself, others, or the world might have been formed during those earlier experiences that are keeping these patterns going? For example, if you consistently find yourself in jobs where you feel undervalued, could this stem from an early SEE where your contributions were dismissed?
- **Fear Inventory:**
  - List your current fears, especially those that hold you back from pursuing your goals or living more fully.
  - For each fear, gently ask: "What past experience might this fear be rooted in?" "Is this fear based on a current, objective reality, or is it just an echo of that uncomfortable past?" This helps to untangle the "illusion" from the present reality. It's like checking if that monster under the bed is actually a monster, or just a pile of clothes.
- **The "Why Don't I?" Inquiry:** Let's revisit that question I often pose: "Why don't you do the things that you know you're supposed to do to accomplish the tasks you believe that you must to have the life you dream about?" Explore how past failures, criticisms, or disappointments might be contributing to this inaction. Is it the fear of repeating a past mistake? Is it a belief formed in the past that you're just not capable? I lived under a bridge and had to scale a wall to find food after losing everything. That was a painful past, but it taught me invaluable lessons about resilience and hunger for success. It etched lessons into me that no classroom ever could.

"Take Back the Power in Your Pain and Use It to Pave the Way for Your Path."

This is the ultimate alchemy, isn't it? Transforming the lead of past pain into the gold of future strength. Your pain, once you've processed and understood it, contains an immense amount of energy. Instead of letting that energy keep you stuck or define you negatively, you can consciously redirect it.

- **Pain as a Motivator:** Let the memory of past struggles fuel your determination to create a truly different future. If you experienced poverty, let that memory drive your ambition for financial security, not just for yourself but perhaps to help others. If you suffered injustice, let that pain ignite a passion for fairness and advocacy. It's about turning your wounds into wisdom.

- **Empathy from Experience:** Your past pains can become a source of profound empathy. Having navigated difficult waters yourself allows you to understand and connect with others who are facing similar challenges. This connection is a powerful gift, allowing you to truly walk in someone else's shoes.

- **Purpose from Hardship:** Sometimes, our deepest purpose is revealed through our greatest struggles. The challenges you've overcome can equip you to guide, teach, or support others on similar journeys. Your "mess" can absolutely become your message. The very things that caused you pain can become the foundation upon which you build a path of meaning and contribution. When I was called names as a kid, it hurt, but that hurt propelled me to become an advocate for those who are different. My financial bankruptcies taught me lessons about business that I now share to help others avoid similar pitfalls. My struggles truly became my textbooks.

Your Past: The Rich Soil of Your Island

Your past, with all its triumphs and traumas, its joys and its sorrows, is not a barren wasteland. It is the rich, complex soil from which your present has grown. By courageously examining it, by reframing its narratives, and by consciously choosing to extract its wisdom and strength, you stop it from being an anchor that holds you back.

It is never too late to act and change your life. Your past experiences, even the most difficult ones, have shaped you, but they do not have to define your limits. They can, instead, inform your strength, deepen their wisdom, and clarify your path forward. Take back the power from your pain. Let the lessons of yesterday pave a more deliberate, purposeful, and powerful way for your tomorrows. Your past is not a life sentence; it is a library of invaluable data waiting to be used to design a future where you not only survive but truly thrive. So go on, open that library, but maybe skip the horror section for a bit. There are far more inspiring stories waiting to be written.

CHAPTER VII
A is for Acknowledge *(Your Fears)*
Befriending the Storms & Fears

"Feed your Faith and Starve your Fears."

Navigating the Inevitable Storms!

So, your "Island of One" – that conscious, unique space you're building – is really taking shape. That's amazing! But here's the thing, even the most beautiful, well-cared-for island is going to hit some rough weather sometimes. And often, those storms show up as fear. The next big step on our journey together is about learning to really *befriend* your fears. It's about transforming them from those paralyzing monsters into helpful guides that actually lead you through life's inevitable challenges and help you grow. As I've said before, "Your fear is just an illusion showing you an assumed future based on an uncomfortable past." Once we truly grasp that it's an illusion, we can start to gently disarm its power.

Understanding Those Five Basic Human Fears and How They Show Up

Fear is such a fundamental human emotion, isn't it? It's wired into us, a primal survival mechanism. While most of us aren't exactly running from saber-toothed tigers these days, that same ancient fear response can still get triggered by all sorts of things we *perceive* as threats, whether they're physical or psychological. Drawing from different ideas about human psychology, like Dr. Karl Albrecht's work on five basic fears, we can start to see the common threads in a lot of what holds us back:

- **Extinction (The Fear of Completely Vanishing):** This is the deepest, most fundamental fear – the fear of death, of not existing anymore. It might sound extreme, but in our daily lives, it can show up as a paralyzing fear of a serious illness, an overwhelming fear of flying, or even a really strong resistance to any kind of change that feels like it threatens our very core sense of self or survival. It's that gut feeling of being erased, either literally or metaphorically.

- **Mutilation (The Fear of Harm or Losing a Part of Ourselves):** This one's all about the fear of physical harm, injury, illness, or anything that feels like it might invade or compromise our body's wholeness. It can show up as a fear of spiders or snakes, a dread of needles or medical procedures, or even just anxiety about getting older and our bodies changing. It's about that fear of our physical integrity being compromised.

I remember the very moment my daughter, Kayla, came into the world, a truly primal fear just *gripped* me. It wasn't the usual new-parent worries about sleepless nights or scraped knees. No, this was a deeply personal terror, born from the very essence of my own being. I was utterly terrified she

CHAPTER VII: A is for Acknowledge (Your Fears)

might be born without fingers, like me. This wasn't just a fleeting worry, a tiny whisper of unease. No, this was a deep, guttural dread, clawing its way up from my core. It was a fear of mutilation so profound, so utterly terrifying, that it felt as though the agony of my own past pain was being physically projected, beam by agonizing beam, onto the innocent, fragile form of my child. The thought wasn't just in my head; it was visceral, a punch to the gut that left me breathless. It was overwhelming, a suffocating blanket of anxiety, thick and heavy, threatening to extinguish the flickering flame of joy that should have blazed brightly with her arrival. Every beat of my heart echoed with that terrifying possibility, every breath I took felt shallow, tainted by this insidious fear that tried to overshadow the miracle of her existence.

- **Loss of Autonomy (The Fear of Being Stuck, Controlled, or Helpless):** This is all about the fear of not being able to control our own lives and choices. It might look like claustrophobia, a fear of commitment (feeling "trapped"), a fear of being micromanaged at work, or even a dread of debt because it feels like financial obligations are controlling you. It's that horrible, stuck-in-quicksand feeling when you're facing overwhelming circumstances.

- **Separation (The Fear of Being Left Alone or Rejected):** We are truly social creatures, aren't we? So, the fear of being cut off from others is incredibly powerful. This manifests as a fear of loneliness, a fear of public speaking (because you're worried about rejection from the audience), a fear of being excluded, or even the terror of a relationship breakup. It's that deep fear of being truly alone, unwanted, or insignificant in the eyes of others.

- **Ego-death (The Fear of Shame, Worthlessness, or Looking Foolish):** This is the fear of losing our sense of self-worth, our identity, or our integrity. It's the fear of looking silly, of being seen as incompetent or inadequate, or failing in a way that truly diminishes how we feel about ourselves. This can show up as performance anxiety, perfectionism (that fear of making mistakes), fear of criticism, or a deep dread of any situation that might expose our perceived flaws and lead to shame. As I've mentioned before, after my bankruptcies, "I felt as if I was smaller than an enigma. I had failed society's pulse." That was a real brush with ego-death, a profound blow to how I saw myself. And in my early dating life, my fear of women seeing my hand led me to become incredibly good at hiding it – a clear manifestation of ego-death, that fear of being judged as "less than."

Understanding these basic fears helps us see that so many of our specific anxieties – like fear of failure, fear of success, fear of change, fear of intimacy – are often just different branches stemming from these deeper roots. When you feel fear, try to gently trace it back: *Which of these core anxieties is it really touching upon for me?* It's like finding out that the monster under your bed was just a pile of clothes. Once you identify the root, it tends to lose some of its power.

Learning to Listen to Fear: It's Not a Barrier, It's a Message

Our natural instinct is usually to pull away from fear, to avoid the thoughts or situations that trigger it. But what if fear wasn't just an enemy to be conquered, but actually a messenger carrying some really valuable information? Imagine it like a slightly dramatic, but ultimately well-meaning, friend sending you a cryptic text.

Fear often signals:

- **An Area That Needs Your Attention or a Little Prep:** If you're scared of public speaking, it might be a message that you need to prepare more thoroughly, practice your delivery, or learn some techniques for managing performance anxiety. If you're nervous about a career change, it might signal the need for more research, skill development, or some financial planning. It's not telling you to stop; it's telling you to get ready.

- **A Growth Edge:** So often, the things we fear most are precisely the things that lie just outside our comfort zone, representing an amazing opportunity for significant personal growth. The fear is actually an indicator that you're pushing your boundaries. It's like that little voice daring you to try the spiciest hot sauce – it's going to be intense, but you might discover a whole new level of flavor (or pain tolerance!).

- **An Unmet Need:** As we talked about in the last chapter, fear can sometimes be a symptom of a core need that isn't being met. Fear of financial instability often points to an unmet need for safety. Fear of loneliness points to an unmet need for connection. Think of fear often as a symptom, not the actual disease itself.

- **A Limiting Belief at Play:** Fear is so often tied to our belief systems (we'll dive deeper into this in Key #7). If you fear failure, it might be connected to a limiting belief that your worth is somehow conditional on your achievements. It's like a warning light flashing, telling you to check your internal programming.

The goal here isn't to try and get rid of fear completely – a life without *any* fear would probably be pretty reckless and short! The real goal is to gently change your relationship with fear. Instead of letting it paralyze you, learn to listen to its message. Ask it: "What are you trying to tell me, fear? What do you want me to pay attention to right now?"

The Hidden Cost of Unchecked Fear: Keeping Your Island Small

When we consistently let fear call the shots in our lives, our world inevitably shrinks. Unchecked fear:

- **Stops You From Taking Risks:** Meaningful growth and true achievement almost always involve some level of risk, don't they? Fear keeps us playing it safe, often stuck in familiar but potentially unfulfilling routines. As I've often asked, "Why don't you do the things you know you should... to experience the life that you dream about?" So often, the answer is just fear. It keeps you cozy, but ultimately confined, in a cage.
- **Muzzles Your Creativity and Innovation:** Fear of judgment or fear of failure can make us really hesitant to try new things, share those unconventional ideas, or simply express our authentic selves. It puts a literal muzzle on your inner genius.
- **Hurts Your Relationships:** Fear of being vulnerable can prevent truly deep connections from forming. Fear of conflict can lead to unspoken issues and resentment. It essentially builds walls between you and the people who care about you most.
- **Leads to Regret:** When people look back on their lives, many regret not the things they did, but the things they were too afraid to do. It's often far worse to look back and wish you had tried, than to have tried and perhaps stumbled a bit. At least you tried.
- **Keeps You Trapped:** Remember that feeling, "You're free to make a decision, but once you have... You can't go back. It's

kind of like Checkpoint Charlie going into East Berlin. Once you're in the middle, your fears lock you into that zone." Unchecked fear truly creates these "no man's lands" in our lives, where we just feel stuck, unable to move forward or backward. It creates a psychological trap, a truly frozen-in-place feeling.

Ultimately, the real cost of unchecked fear is a smaller, less vibrant life. It keeps the boundaries of your "Island of One" constricted, stopping you from truly exploring its full potential and experiencing all the richness that lies just beyond your current comfort zone. As Franklin D. Roosevelt famously said, "The only thing we have to fear is fear itself." Because the fear of fear is often the real killer of dreams.

Let's Get Practical: Befriending Your Fears

Befriending your fear doesn't mean you have to *like* it; it simply means understanding it, learning to manage it, and not letting it be the only thing driving your decisions. Think of it like training a rather energetic, unruly pet – you don't get rid of it, you just teach it how to behave around you.

Simple Techniques for Handling Anxiety and Fear When It Shows Up

- **Mindfulness and Breathwork:** When fear pops up, it often kicks off that physical stress response – racing heart, shallow breathing. Mindfulness practices *(like simply focusing on what you can sense around you, or a calming guided meditation)* and deliberate, slow breathing techniques can really calm your nervous system. They create a little bit of space between the fearful trigger and your automatic reaction. I've faced moments where that physical response was absolutely screaming.

I vividly remember one beautiful winter day, my family and I were flying our airplane up to Big Bear, a quick mountain flight from Southern California. The kids were all excited for sledding, happily wearing their headsets, coloring in the back, totally oblivious to the pilot (that's me!) trying to be cool in the front. I was feeling great, enjoying the view, chatting away like a happy pilot. We were on final approach, just a few feet above the runway, ready to touch down, when my eyes scanned the cockpit. Three green lights... where were the three green lights for the landing gear? My heart *jumped* into my throat, exactly like they say. The primitive brain wanted to panic, to just freeze or scream. Every fiber of my being screamed danger! But years of training, of drilling checklists and emergency procedures, just kicked in. The fight-or-flight response, instead of leading to paralysis or a wild, uncontrolled reaction, channeled into a very precise sequence. It was almost automatic: slam the landing gear switch down, go to full throttle, and push the nose up for a go-around.

There's a tricky tree line right off the end of that runway at Big Bear. The gear just touched the ground for an instant as it came down, within an inch of where it would have landed without them fully extended. The plane momentarily settled, then roared back to life, the engine protesting slightly but responding, and we climbed away. We cleared that ridgeline by what felt like inches, though it was probably more.

The kids, thankfully, were oblivious, still lost in their coloring, probably just wondering why Daddy suddenly stomped on the gas so hard. We circled around, I pulled myself together, made the checklists, and landed safely a few minutes later, much more deliberately. They went sledding that afternoon, completely unaware of how close we came to a very different ending. That experience wasn't just a near-miss; it was a visceral lesson in the power of conscious response over instinctual panic. It showed me how critical it is to have those calm-inducing techniques, those practiced drills, so ingrained that they can override the primal scream of fear. It taught me that while the fear is real and unavoidable in certain moments, your reaction to it is a choice you can train yourself to control. And trust me, after that, I paid a lot more attention to those pre-landing checklists! It solidified the understanding that a moment of intense fear isn't an invitation to collapse, but a signal to execute.

That incident taught me a lesson I would never forget. Flying is a skill that, if I didn't dedicate the time to it constantly, I shouldn't be in the plane. I ended up selling that plane shortly after that day. I waited several years before buying another airplane and stayed focused on my true passion. Today, I fly weekly, with a renewed appreciation for deliberate practice.

- **Cognitive Reframing (Questioning Those Fearful Thoughts):** This is about challenging those fearful thoughts, not just generally, but by really picking apart the assumptions underneath them. If you're terrified of presenting to investors, for example, it's not *just* the public speaking that's the problem. Dig a little deeper: Is it the fear of looking foolish (ego-death)? The fear of losing control over your vision (loss of autonomy)? Or the fear of rejection, and what that might imply about your worth? By pinpointing the core fear, you can start to reframe it. Instead of thinking, "I'm going to mess up and they'll think I'm incompetent," you can gently shift to, "This is an opportunity to showcase my competence and passion. Even if there are tough questions,

they're just part of the process of growth." This shift moves you from a defensive, fear-driven mindset to a proactive, opportunity-focused one.
  - **Identify the Fearful Thought:** "If I give this presentation, I'll mess up and everyone will think I'm incompetent."
  - **Examine the Evidence:** What's the *actual* evidence for this thought? And what's the evidence *against* it? Have you given successful presentations before? Have you learned from past mistakes?
  - **Challenge Catastrophic Thinking:** What's the absolute *worst* that could happen, really? How likely is that? How would you cope if it did? What's the *best* that could happen? What's the most *realistic* outcome? Sometimes, the "worst-case scenario" is just a comedy of errors playing out in your head, not a real threat.
  - **Create an Alternative, More Balanced Thought:** "I'm nervous about the presentation, but I've prepared well. Even if I stumble a bit, it's a learning experience, and most people are supportive. I've got this."
- **Exposure (Little Steps Towards the Scary Thing):** For very specific fears or anxieties, gradually and safely exposing yourself to the feared situation in tiny, manageable steps can really reduce the fear response over time. (For big phobias, this is often best done with a professional guide.) Think of it like getting used to cold water – you don't just jump into the Arctic Ocean; you wade in slowly, allowing your body to adjust. In a business setting, if you dread networking, start with one small, low-stakes interaction – maybe a quick chat with just one person at an event, rather than diving headfirst into a crowded room demanding you work it like a pro. Each small step builds confidence for the next.
- **Visualization for Success:** Close your eyes and mentally rehearse successfully navigating the feared situation.

Visualize yourself feeling calm, confident, and achieving your desired outcome. This can really help build positive associations and ease that pre-event anxiety. Before a big meeting or a difficult conversation, play out the best-case scenario in your mind in vivid detail. See yourself speaking clearly, handling any challenges gracefully, and reaching the desired outcome. Engage all your senses. This mental rehearsal actually pre-wires your brain for success, making the actual event feel more familiar and less daunting.

Building Your Courage Muscle, One Step at a Time

Courage isn't about *not* being afraid; it's about acting *despite* the fear. You build courage just like you build a muscle – through consistent, gentle practice. You wouldn't expect to deadlift 500 pounds on your very first try, right?

- **Spot Your Comfort Zone:** What activities, situations, or conversations do you usually avoid because of fear or discomfort? Be kind, but honest, about your current boundaries.
- **Take Tiny, Purposeful Steps:** Choose one small action that pushes you just a little bit outside your comfort zone. If you fear social situations, it might be as simple as striking up a brief conversation with a cashier. If public speaking is your fear, maybe volunteer to speak up for one minute in a small, safe group meeting. In business, this might mean taking on a small project that stretches your skills, rather than waiting for the "perfect" multi-million dollar opportunity. Each small, brave step is like adding a brick to the strong foundation of your courage.
- **Acknowledge and Celebrate Those Small Wins:** Every single time you act despite fear, pause and really acknowledge your courage. This helps reinforce that positive behavior. Give yourself a mental high-five, or maybe even an actual cookie!

Celebrating these small victories isn't about ego; it's about gently conditioning your brain to associate discomfort with growth and reward.
- **Reflect and Learn:** After you've stepped out of your comfort zone, take a moment to reflect on the experience. What did you learn from it? Was it as bad as you feared? How can you apply this learning next time? This reflection loop is so critical for turning experience into wisdom and making sure that each challenging moment truly contributes to your growing resilience.

"Feed Your Faith and Starve Your Fears."

This powerful principle is all about consciously shifting your focus. Fear and faith (whether it's faith in yourself, in a higher power, in your plan, or in your ability to cope) are like two wolves battling within you. The one you feed is the one that wins.

- **Focus on Your Strengths and Resources (Your Gifts - Key #1):** Gently remind yourself of past challenges you've successfully overcome. My father's powerful lesson to "never give up" and "never surrender," echoing the poem he shared with my daughter Savanna, truly became my mantra through business failures and personal struggles. When faced with a looming deadline or a difficult client, I don't focus on the potential for failure; I lean into my innate problem-solving ability and my tenacity, knowing I've navigated tougher waters before.
- **Focus on Your Plan and Purpose (Key #4):** Let your "why" be bigger and bolder than your fear. If your purpose is strong enough, it will gently pull you through those moments of doubt and discomfort. My desire to provide for my family, to ensure they experienced the world in new ways (like those airplane trips!), was a purpose far stronger than any fear of failure. It was the lighthouse guiding me through the fog.

- **Practice Gratitude:** Simply focusing on what you have and what's going well in your life can really counteract fear's tendency to highlight what's wrong or missing. A daily gratitude practice can fundamentally shift your perspective, making you less susceptible to the draining pull of fear.
- **Use Affirmations:** Create positive statements that actively counteract your fearful thoughts and strengthen your belief in your ability to succeed (we'll talk more about this in Key #7). For example: "I am capable and resilient. I can handle this challenge." I often tell myself, "I will not go quietly into that good night. I will rage against the dying of the light." This isn't just poetry; it's a powerful affirmation of defiance against fear and limitations, a powerful declaration of intention that actually reprograms the subconscious.
- **Let Music Be Your Guide: "Fear" by Blue October:** Speaking of powerful tools for courage, I'm reminded of a song that holds a special place in my heart, and maybe yours too: "Fear" by Blue October. It's a song I know and connect with deeply, playing it during those "love sessions" with my guitar. That's a beautiful way to engage with music, allowing it to be a channel for your own emotions and reflection.

The band's frontman, Justin Furstenfeld, has been incredibly open about his own journey through struggles like addiction, depression, and bipolar disorder. His music, especially on the album "Sway," where "Fear" is found, comes from a place of raw honesty and a powerful shift towards optimism after getting sober. "Fear" really embodies that spirit of moving past self-doubt and guilt. It's about recognizing that you don't *have* to be afraid, that you can ask for help, and that your past doesn't define who you are now. In a world often filled with "perfect" online images, Blue October's music, and "Fear" in particular, bravely acknowledges the messiness and the real struggles behind the scenes. It becomes an anthem for "recovering from oneself," finding that sense of being "mended" even when things feel uncomfortable. When you play it on your guitar, you're not just playing notes; you're resonating with that message of confronting your own difficult feelings and finding a path forward, creating your own harmony out of the struggle. It's a testament to how art can give us words and feelings for our own journeys of courage.

Befriending your fears is an ongoing journey, truly. It's about recognizing fear as a natural, human part of the experience, learning to listen to its messages without being completely controlled by them, and consistently choosing courage over comfort. As you do this, you'll find that the storms won't disappear, but your ability to navigate them with grace and strength will expand dramatically, allowing your "Island of One" to flourish beautifully, even in turbulent seas.

CHAPTER VIII

S is for Satisfy *(Your Needs)*
Honoring Your Core Needs

"True fulfillment comes not from accumulating things or experiences that society deems desirable, but from authentically meeting the fundamental requirements of your being."

You know, true fulfillment isn't about chasing after all the shiny things the world tells us we *should* want. It's actually a much deeper, more personal journey: it's about genuinely tending to what truly nourishes *you*, at your core.

Fueling Your Personal Ecosystem

Ever tried to set off on a really long road trip without thinking about gas? No matter how perfect your map is, or how excitedly you've packed, you won't get very far, right? Eventually, your car's just going to sputter to a stop, leaving you a bit stranded. This is such a perfect way to think about our own lives, especially when we're trying to achieve something big. To keep going, to avoid that frustrating feeling of burnout, we *all* need to refuel, to get that continuous replenishment. Without those crucial "stops," even our most brilliant plans and hardest work can just run out of steam before we hit our destination.

Think about a vibrant island ecosystem – it needs just the right blend of sunshine, water, and rich soil to really flourish. Well, your own personal ecosystem, your "Island of One," is exactly the same. It absolutely needs its fundamental human needs to be met to truly thrive. Ignoring them is kind of like trying to sail a magnificent ship with empty fuel tanks; you're not going to get anywhere, no matter how amazing your captaining skills are! This chapter is all about getting cozy with what those core needs actually are, and then figuring out, together, how to truly weave their fulfillment into the fabric of your life.

Understanding What You Really Need: A Little Chat About Human Needs

My dad, bless his heart, loved introducing me and my siblings to all sorts of fascinating people with incredibly fresh ways of looking at life. And honestly, this next bit is totally thanks to that spirit. I'm just here to share what I've learned, not to be a psychology professor, but to have a real talk about something pretty profound.

So, there was this psychologist, Abraham Maslow. He came up with this really insightful idea, often shown as a pyramid, that he called the "Hierarchy of Needs." It basically suggests that we need to get our most basic needs taken care of – things like food and safety – before we can even begin to think about those higher-level desires for love, feeling good about ourselves, and ultimately, truly becoming the fullest version of who we're meant to be.

Let's break it down simply, almost like layers of a cake:

- **Physiological Needs:** These are the absolute basics, the non-negotiables for just being alive: air, food, water, a safe place to sleep, clothes, feeling warm. Seriously, try to think clearly when you're starving or shivering – it's practically impossible! Your body just can't function its best.
- **Safety Needs:** Once those basic "survival" needs are mostly met, our minds naturally shift to feeling secure and safe. This means things like having a stable job, enough resources, good health, and a safe home. Think of it like finally finding a calm, secure harbor for your island.
- **Love and Belongingness Needs:** When you feel physically safe, the next big thing our hearts yearn for is connection. This is all about relationships – friendship, intimacy, trust, feeling accepted, both giving and receiving affection and love. We're wired for this, deep down. We need our tribe.
- **Esteem Needs:** Maslow kind of split these into two: first, feeling good about *yourself* (like having dignity, achieving things, feeling capable, being independent), and second, wanting to be respected by others (things like status or prestige). It's about that warm feeling of knowing your own worth and having others acknowledge it too.
- **Self-Actualization Needs:** This is the tippy-top of Maslow's pyramid, and it's all about reaching your full potential, finding self-fulfillment, really growing as a person, and having those incredible "peak experiences." Maslow described it as wanting to accomplish everything you possibly can, to become the absolute most you can be. It's about blossoming into the most authentic, vibrant *you*.

Now, while Maslow's pyramid is super helpful, there are other cool ways to look at our needs too. For example, some theories, like Self-Determination Theory, highlight our needs for **autonomy** (feeling in control of our own lives), **competence** (feeling effective and capable), and **relatedness** (feeling connected to others). And then there's Tony Robbins, who talks about six human needs: **Certainty, Uncertainty/Variety, Significance, Love/Connection, Growth, and Contribution.**

The common thread weaving through all these ideas is this: we're not just here to survive. We're driven by this deep, natural desire to grow, to connect, to give back, and to express the unique person we are. As I've often said, "God already gave what you need to do what He wants to do." It really points to this beautiful truth that we inherently have the capacity to meet these needs, or at least to earnestly strive for them. Our real job is to become aware of what those needs are and then gently, deliberately create a life where they can truly flourish. As the poet Rumi so beautifully put it, "What you seek is seeking you." It's like your true needs are already out there, just waiting for you to recognize them.

Real Needs vs. Fleeting Wants: A Crucial Distinction

In today's world, it's so incredibly easy to mix up what we *truly need* with what we just *think we want*. Wants are often these quick, shiny distractions, usually pushed on us from the outside, and they only give us a super brief burst of happiness. Needs, on the other hand, are fundamental, they come from deep within, and when we meet them, it brings a real, lasting sense of well-being. It's a bit like the difference between a sugar rush and a truly nourishing meal.

Let's think about some examples together:
- **Want:** "I really want the newest smartphone."
  - **Possible Deeper Need:** Maybe it's a need for

Connection (to stay in touch with loved ones), or
  Competence (to feel capable with the latest tech), or
  even **Esteem** (to feel relevant and up-to-date).
- **Want:** "I've gotta have that luxury car."
    - **Possible Deeper Need:** Could it be **Safety** (wanting a truly reliable vehicle), **Significance** (using it as a status symbol), or even **Certainty** (dependable transportation)?
- **Want:** "I want to be famous on social media!"
    - **Possible Deeper Need:** This might hint at **Love/Connection** (to be liked and followed), **Significance** (to feel important), or even a slightly twisted version of **Contribution** (to share a message, even if it feels superficial).

The sneaky danger here is that we can get so caught up in chasing these surface-level desires that we never truly understand the deeper, often hidden, needs that are actually fueling them. We become experts at spotting what we *want* – the cool gadget, the fancy car, the growing online presence – but we often fail to dig down and discover the underlying void we're honestly trying to fill.

Take the smartphone, for instance. It's a marvel of connection, putting the world at our fingertips. But simply buying it doesn't automatically give us a sense of belonging or genuine connection, does it? In fact, for many of us, that constant stream of notifications and the picture-perfect online lives we see can actually make us feel *more* isolated and inadequate. We got the *want* (the smartphone), but the deeper *need* (for real human connection) often stays unmet.

And then there's the magnetic pull of a luxury car. It promises so much more than just getting from A to B – it hints at status, freedom, and an undeniable thrill. I'm certainly no stranger to

CHAPTER VIII: S is for Satisfy (Your Needs) Honoring Your Core Needs

this! Over the years, I've had the immense privilege of owning a pretty extensive collection of high-performance and luxury vehicles. Three different Ferraris have graced my garage, each a symphony of power and exquisite design. A BMW i8, with its futuristic lines, offered a glimpse into cutting-edge automotive engineering. My collection has also included a precise Porsche, several luxurious and dependable Mercedes-Benz models, and even a classic 1962 Chrysler 300, a beautiful piece of American automotive history. Honestly, if you can name a significant luxury or performance car, chances are, at some point, it's been part of my journey.

And for me, this pursuit isn't just about collecting; it's about truly appreciating the absolute pinnacle of engineering and design, and that pure exhilaration these machines can deliver. But here's the thing: parking that gleaming machine in your driveway doesn't magically erase a deep-seated insecurity. That fleeting surge of pride might cover up underlying self-doubt for a moment, but that core feeling often just lingers, waiting for the next external validation to temporarily soothe it. The *strategy* (the luxury car) was used, but the core *need* (for genuine self-worth) was still left unaddressed.

And what about that intoxicating chase for followers, likes, and shares in the digital world? The numbers climb, the notifications ping, and for a fleeting moment, you might feel seen, heard, significant. Yet, behind the screen, that quiet gnawing feeling of insignificance can stubbornly persist. The virtual applause, while momentarily satisfying, often doesn't translate into a real sense of purpose or intrinsic value. Getting those followers (the *want*) didn't truly meet the *need* (for meaning and validation that honestly has to come from within).

This big disconnect between our wants and our needs is a bit like trying to quench a profound thirst with a rich, delicious dessert. That dessert, with all its amazing flavors and satisfying textures, might give you a momentary burst of pleasure, a lovely distraction. It might even briefly feel like it's helping your thirst because it has some moisture. But it utterly fails to provide the fundamental hydration your body *truly* requires. You got the dessert you wanted, but the essential biological need for water remains unsatisfied, leading to continued dehydration and, eventually, an even deeper yearning. The danger, then, isn't necessarily in the wants themselves, but in how easily they can distract us from the vital work of figuring out and fulfilling our *true*, underlying needs.

I'll never forget the day I splurged on those $1,000 Louis Vuitton shoes. It wasn't about the practical side of footwear; it was about the unspoken promise they seemed to whisper. I *wanted* to feel a certain way – maybe a rush of confidence, a sense of belonging to some exclusive club, or a validation of my own worth. It was a subtle, almost unconscious attempt to fill an unmet need for status, for significance, for something intangible that I genuinely believed those opulent shoes could provide.

But that fleeting thrill of the purchase? It faded pretty quickly. As I wore them, the initial glow of perceived prestige dulled, revealing the stark truth: I was chasing a want, not truly satisfying a fundamental need. The shoes were an expensive, momentary distraction, a luxurious veil draped over a deeper yearning. They offered a brief sense of elevation, but they couldn't address the underlying hunger for genuine fulfillment or self-acceptance. That whole experience served as a potent, though costly, lesson: real contentment doesn't live in the fleeting acquisition of material desires but in truly understanding and addressing the authentic needs that lie beneath them.

When We Ignore What We Really Need: The Hidden Costs

When our core needs consistently go unmet, they don't just magically disappear. Instead, they create this internal tension, a kind of subtle sabotage that can quietly undermine our best efforts to truly thrive. This can show up in so many ways:

- **Feeling Constantly Stressed and Anxious:** If our safety needs aren't met (like worrying about money, having an unstable home, or health concerns), it can lead to this persistent worry, like being on high alert all the time. My family experienced this firsthand when our business hit some serious rough patches financially. I remember working 18-hour days, just absolutely driven by this intense desire to get us back to solid ground and ensure my family felt safe. When your "ship sinks," as I've said, you instinctively go back to basics. And when those basics are threatened, your body and mind definitely let you know.
- **Relationship Wobbles:** If our needs for love, connection, and belonging aren't nurtured, it can lead to feelings of loneliness, or even unhealthy relationship patterns where we either push people away or become overly clingy. All because that fundamental need isn't getting the attention it deserves.
- **Low Self-Esteem and "Can't Be Bothered" Feelings:** When our esteem needs are neglected (feeling incompetent, unappreciated, or like we lack purpose), it can really chip away at our confidence and make it incredibly hard to even start pursuing our goals. If you don't feel good about yourself, why even try, right?
- **Unhealthy Habits Creeping In:** Sometimes, we try to meet our legitimate needs through behaviors that aren't actually good for us in the long run. For example:
    - Trying to find **certainty** through being overly controlling or rigid.

- ○ Seeking **significance** by being arrogant or constantly craving attention.
- ○ Looking for **connection** by being clingy or always trying to please everyone.
- ○ Seeking **comfort** (from unmet safety or love needs) by overeating, using substances, or excessive escapism (like falling into a Netflix binge, which we've all been there for!). It's a temporary patch that unfortunately just makes the original problem worse.
- **Burnout and Feeling Stuck:** When our needs for growth and contribution aren't met, it can lead to this profound sense of emptiness, boredom, and a feeling that life just lacks meaning, even if other needs seem to be doing okay. You might be "existing" but not truly "living."

Ignoring your core needs is kind of like driving a car with the emergency brake halfway on. You might still inch forward, but it's going to take a ton of effort, be super inefficient, and eventually, things are going to break down. Making real progress on your "Thrive Plan" will feel like an uphill battle until these fundamental requirements are gently and deliberately addressed. As Plato wisely said, "The greatest wealth is to live content with little." True richness really comes from within, not from what we acquire to try and cover up what's missing.

Let's Get Practical: How to Honor Your Needs

Honoring your core needs is truly an ongoing, gentle practice of becoming more aware of yourself and then taking deliberate steps. It's about figuring out what you genuinely need and then thoughtfully arranging your life to provide it.

A Little Self-Check-in: What Do You Need Most Right Now?

The "Needs Inventory" Exercise:

- Grab a piece of paper or open a note on your phone.
- Think about those core human needs we just chatted about (like Physiological, Safety, Love/Belonging, Esteem, Self-Actualization from Maslow; or Certainty, Variety, Significance, Connection, Growth, Contribution from Robbins).
- For each one, just quickly rate how met it feels for you right now, on a scale of 1 (Nope, not at all met) to 10 (Feeling totally fulfilled here!).
- Then, look for the 2-3 needs with the lowest scores. These are probably the ones that are asking for a little extra love and attention right now.
- For each of those low-scoring needs, maybe spend a few minutes journaling or just thinking:
  - How is this unmet need showing up for you today? (What thoughts are you having? What feelings? What behaviors are you noticing?)
  - Are there any past experiences that might have contributed to this need feeling a bit neglected?
  - Are you chasing any "wants" right now that might secretly be an attempt to fill this specific void?

The "Frustration to Need" Detective Work:

- The next time you feel frustrated, stressed, angry, or just generally unfulfilled, pause for a moment.
- Ask yourself: "What core need is *not* being met in this situation?" For example, if you're feeling frustrated at work, it might point to a need for more competence, or more autonomy, or more significance. If you're feeling lonely, it's pretty clearly flagging a need for connection. This is really at the heart of truly understanding what drives us – realizing that almost every desire or longing is ultimately serving a fundamental human need. What is this feeling *really* trying to

tell you?

Simple Ways to Nurture Your Needs on Your "Island of One" Journey

Once you've spotted your primary unmet needs, let's brainstorm some healthy, authentic ways to meet them.

For Safety/Certainty:

- Maybe create a simple budget or start building a small emergency fund. It doesn't have to be perfect, just a start.
- Develop some comforting routines that bring you a sense of stability. I start every single morning with prayer, asking to see my blind spots and be more open. This little routine truly helps me feel a sense of spiritual and mental safety before the day even begins, really anchoring my mind.
- Nourish your body through healthier eating and some gentle movement.
- Declutter your physical space a bit. Creating some order can bring a surprising sense of control.

For Love/Connection/Belonging:

- Make a point to schedule quality time with the people you love. My family, especially my girls and my incredible wife Sofia, are my "open and free area," where I feel most comfortable and connected. Honestly, everything I do revolves around them; they are my absolute anchor.
- Consider joining a group or community that shares something you're passionate about.
- Practice active listening and empathy in your conversations – giving connection often brings it right back to you.
- Maybe volunteer or offer a helping hand to someone.
- Set healthy boundaries. Protecting your emotional energy is a huge act of self-love.

For Significance/Esteem:

- Set and celebrate small, achievable goals. Every little win counts!
- Take a moment to truly acknowledge your accomplishments, no matter how tiny. Give yourself some genuine credit!
- Learn a new skill, just for the joy of building competence.
- Identify your unique strengths (remember Key #1?) and look for ways to put them to good use.
- Engage in activities where you can see your contribution. When I talk about being able to "steal first base and hit the ball faster and harder than you can" despite having only one hand, it's not about bragging; it's an expression of the esteem I've built through mastering my own unique way of doing things and truly adapting my gifts. It's about showing what I *can* do, not focusing on limitations.

For Growth/Self-Actualization:

- Pick up a book, sign up for a fun online course, or just explore new ideas that spark your curiosity. I'm always looking into new programs and business ideas, and I check Google Trends every single day to understand what the world is "breathing." It's all about continuous learning, staying curious, and expanding your horizons.
- Gently step out of your comfort zone every now and then.
- Explore hobbies and passions that truly challenge and inspire you.
- Engage in reflective practices like journaling or quiet meditation.

For Contribution:

- Look for ways to help others, share your unique gifts, or make a positive impact, no matter how small it feels.
- Maybe mentor someone who's just starting out.

- Support a cause that truly resonates with you. My work now, sharing what I've learned about business and life with others, really helps me fulfill that deep need for transcendence – to give back and help others find their own path to self-actualization. It's truly one of the most rewarding feelings.

A Personal "Needs-Based" Decision Filter

Before you make any big decisions or commitments, it's incredibly helpful to consciously run them through the filter of your core needs.

Ask yourself:

- "Will this choice genuinely help me meet one or more of my core needs in a healthy, authentic way?"
- "Could this choice potentially compromise or sabotage one of my important needs?"
- "Am I making this decision because it's truly connected to a deep need, or is it just a superficial want?"

For example, before taking on a demanding new project at work, pause and consider if it will truly support your need for growth and significance, or if it might overwhelm you and mess with your need for safety (like a healthy work-life balance or your overall health). Before making a big purchase, honestly assess if it meets a genuine need or if it's just an attempt to satisfy a want that's actually masking a deeper, unmet need.

By consistently honoring your core needs, you're essentially building a fertile, nurturing ecosystem right there on your "Island of One." This inner stability and nourishment provide all the energy and resilience you'll need to pursue your "Thrive Plan" with real vigor and to navigate life's inevitable challenges from a place of genuine strength and authenticity. You stop running on fumes and start fueling your journey from deep within. And honestly, that's a much, much better place to be.

CHAPTER IX

S is for Strengthen *(Your Beliefs)*
Reshaping Your Needs

"Yes... you can change your belief to get where you want to go."

Have you ever thought about your mind like an amazing supercomputer? It's constantly running on its own unique software—your personal belief systems. And you know how it goes with computers, right? Over time, that software can get a little dusty, sometimes bogged down with tiny glitches, or even have some hidden "bugs" that quietly mess with your flow and happiness. So, a huge, beautiful part of what we're going to explore here is like giving your whole system a loving upgrade, carefully smoothing out those kinks, or maybe, just maybe, bravely deciding it's time to install a completely new operating system altogether! This isn't about little adjustments; it's about a deep, heartfelt transformation of the very programs that shape how you see the world, how you respond to things, and ultimately, the reality you experience. It's about tenderly choosing to embrace beliefs that lift you up, that feel more true and expansive, so they can truly be your allies as you navigate all the wonderful complexities of life.

If your "Island of One" has its unique shores, a vibrant ecosystem, and a path you're bravely charting, then imagine this: your beliefs are truly its beating heart, its operating system. They're that invisible, quiet software running in the background, gently processing every experience, whispering guidance for every decision, and ultimately, crafting the beautiful reality you perceive and inhabit. As I often share, "You're not born with beliefs... you create your own beliefs. And those truths that you've decided become the walls you put up around yourself." This conversation is about understanding this beautiful architecture within you and learning how we can lovingly upgrade your operating system so you can truly flourish. It's about shifting from just passively receiving the "programming" you might have picked up along the way, especially when you were little, to becoming the mindful, deliberate programmer of your own precious mind. You get to lovingly decide what code guides your life.

How Your Core Beliefs (Both Conscious and Unconscious) Gently Take Shape and Color Your View of Life

So, let's chat about these "core beliefs." What are they, really? They're those deeply held assumptions, those quiet convictions, and the fundamental "truths" we carry about ourselves, about others, and about the beautiful, intricate dance of the world. They don't just appear overnight, do they? Instead, they're built so carefully over time, layer by gentle layer, through a tapestry of really powerful influences:

CHAPTER IX: S is for Strengthen (Your Beliefs) Reshaping Your Beliefs

- **Early Childhood Experiences:** Ah, these are truly the foundation, aren't they? All those early interactions with parents, caregivers, teachers, and siblings during our most impressionable years send such potent messages about whether we're worthy of love, what we're capable of, how safe the world feels, and what we can gently expect from relationships. Can you picture a little one who's always lovingly praised for their effort? They might blossom into believing, "I am capable." But a child who's often met with criticism? They might quietly internalize a feeling of "I'm not good enough." The very emotional atmosphere of our early home—whether it was a haven of security and warmth, or perhaps a place of tension and unpredictability—profoundly shapes our foundational beliefs about safety and trust. It's truly like the earliest code, so tenderly written into your system.

- **Significant Emotional Events (SEEs):** Remember our chats about "Reclaiming Your Past" and "The Captain's Choice"? Well, impactful positive or challenging events can act like a powerful imprint, either gently affirming beliefs you already hold or, sometimes, dramatically shifting them. That "one-handed-monkey" taunt wasn't just a mean comment; it was an SEE that *could* have painfully installed a belief like "I am deficient and different in a bad way." Conversely, a moment of unexpected kindness when you were feeling vulnerable, or a significant personal achievement against all odds, can lovingly forge empowering beliefs about human goodness or your own amazing resilience. These are the moments that leave such a deep, lasting mark on our hearts.

- **Cultural and Societal Conditioning:** From the moment we're born, we're simply immersed in a vast ocean of cultural stories and societal expectations. Messages from media (TV, movies, social media), school, religious communities, and the broader cultural norms subtly and overtly whisper to us what's considered "good" or "bad," "normal" or "different," "possible" or "impossible." Beliefs about success, gender roles, body image, and even money are often absorbed without us even realizing it, from this ever-present cultural soup. It's like that constant, gentle background hum of what society tells us to believe.

- **Repetitive Thoughts and Self-Talk:** That gentle, ongoing conversation you have with yourself—the stories you lovingly tell yourself about who you are, what you've experienced, and what life means—really strengthens your existing beliefs or helps new ones gently take root. If you consistently whisper to yourself, "I always mess things up," that thought pattern, repeated often enough, can quietly solidify into a core belief, even if all the objective evidence lovingly points in another direction. Your inner monologue is truly a powerful programmer for your heart.

- **Interpretations of Experiences:** This is so deeply important: it's not just the raw experiences themselves, but *how we tenderly interpret them* that cements our beliefs. Two beautiful souls can go through a very similar tough event—say, a job loss—and form entirely different beliefs based on their interpretation. One might conclude, "I'm a failure, and I'll never find good work again," while another might gently interpret it as, "This is a setback, but it's an opportunity to find a more fulfilling career." As I've shared, "Every decision I've made is based on how I experienced it, not the truth. They're not always the same." Our interpretations are those unique, heartfelt filters we apply to make meaning.

CHAPTER IX: S is for Strengthen (Your Beliefs) Reshaping Your Beliefs

Many, if not most, of our core beliefs live quietly in our unconscious or subconscious mind. We might not even be consciously aware they exist or where they came from, yet they profoundly and pervasively shape how we see things, how we feel, and what we do. They act like an invisible filter, a personalized lens, through which we gently interpret every single piece of incoming information from the world around us. If you secretly hold a core belief that "people can't be trusted," you will likely interpret ambiguous actions from others—a delayed message, a slightly critical comment—through that cautious lens, readily finding confirmation for your distrust, even where none was ever intended. If you believe "I'm not good enough," you will inevitably filter your achievements and feedback through this lens, gently dismissing praise as politeness or luck, and magnifying any perceived failure or criticism as definitive proof of your inadequacy.

So, your beliefs don't just passively reflect your reality; they actively and continuously *create* it, my dear friend. They are the engine in a powerful, gentle feedback loop:

- Your Beliefs (e.g., "I am unlovable") gently generate...
- Your Thoughts (e.g., "They're probably just being nice to me; they don't really like me.") which tenderly trigger...
- Your Feelings (e.g., Sadness, insecurity, anxiety in social situations) which then gently guide...
- Your Actions (e.g., Withdrawing, avoiding intimacy, acting defensively or needy) which ultimately lead to...
- Your Results (e.g., Difficulty forming deep connections, experiencing rejection), which then, so sadly, seem to reinforce the original belief ("See? I told you I was unlovable.").

This cycle can feel incredibly difficult to break, can't it? Unless we become tenderly aware of the underlying beliefs that are driving it. It's like being caught in a dream, and the very first step to waking up is simply realizing you're dreaming.

Gently Uncovering the Limiting Beliefs That Quietly Restrict Your Potential

Limiting beliefs are like "invisible fences" that gently, yet effectively, guide you within a certain area on your "Island of One." They are those self-imposed boundaries, often masquerading as undeniable truths, that quietly define the perceived limits of what's possible for you, what you truly deserve, and who you can beautifully become. You can't literally see these fences, but you will inevitably feel them—experiencing a gentle resistance, a whisper of fear, or that quiet sense of being "stuck"—whenever you try to grow, make meaningful changes, or bravely step outside your familiar comfort zone. It's like trying to walk through a doorway that your amazing brain is convinced isn't even there.

These invisible fences can be constructed from a wide array of limiting thoughts, often falling into common, understandable categories:

- **Beliefs about Yourself (Your Identity and Capabilities):** These are perhaps the most tender and potent, aren't they? Examples include: "I'm not smart enough to pursue that dream," "I'm inherently unlovable, so I'll always be alone," "I don't truly deserve success or happiness," "I'm too old to start something new / too young to be taken seriously," "I'm just not a creative person, so why even try?" "I'm fundamentally flawed," "I'm a born procrastinator." For years, I gently avoided dating because I was so afraid women would notice my hand and quietly reject me. That was a huge "invisible fence" built from a limiting belief about my own worth and attractiveness. I literally became "good at the art of hiding it" to avoid that perceived judgment, spending so much precious energy on concealment.

- **Beliefs about Others (People and Relationships):** These lovingly color your interactions and expectations. Examples include: "People will always let you down in the end," "You can't truly trust anyone but yourself," "People are inherently selfish and only look out for number one," "If I show my true self, people will reject me," "Relationships are too much hard work and always end in pain."

- **Beliefs about The World/Life in General (The Nature of Reality):** These gently shape your overall outlook and how you approach life's beautiful challenges. Examples: "Life is an endless struggle, and you just have to accept it," "Opportunities are scarce, and you have to fight for every scrap," "The world is a fundamentally dangerous and unfair place," "You have to work incredibly hard and sacrifice everything just to get by," "Things will never get better for people like me."

As I gently mentioned earlier, and it truly bears repeating, "you believe things you assume to be true that really are just assumptions you created from your past experiences." These assumptions, often formed in childhood or during emotionally charged moments and then left unexamined, can gently harden over time into rigid beliefs that effectively fence you in, limiting your choices and your perception of available paths.

I remember a truly painful moment when the Orange County Register, a major local newspaper, published a colossal picture of my face, emblazoned with the single, devastating word: "failure." It felt like a public branding, a scarlet letter for my professional life, after one of my business ventures collapsed. My gut reaction was pure, unadulterated rage. I remember the immediate urge to lash out, to defend my reputation, which quickly led me to contact my attorney, ready to demand a full retraction. I wanted that word, that image, wiped from existence.

However, as the initial storm of emotion gently subsided, a more profound realization began to surface within me. It wasn't the word "failure" itself that truly inflicted the wound; it was my deeply ingrained belief about what "failure" fundamentally *represented*. For so long, I had equated it with an endpoint, a definitive judgment of worthlessness, a sign of personal inadequacy. This ingrained perspective was the *real* source of my agony.

Upon closer inspection of the article—a detail I had initially overlooked in my fury—I discovered the crucial nuance: "failure sowed the seeds of his success." This seemingly small addition was a monumental reframe, a complete recalibration of my perspective. It allowed me to see that setbacks are not brick walls but merely stepping stones, essential components on the path to growth and ultimate achievement. This shift wasn't just a minor adjustment; it was a massive overhaul of my entire operating system, a fundamental change in how I processed and interpreted my experiences. What began as a moment of profound public humiliation, a devastating blow to my ego, was transformed into a powerful affirmation of resilience, a testament to the fact that even in the ashes of perceived defeat, the seeds of future triumph are being sown.

The pivotal takeaway from this experience, and indeed, from navigating any significant challenge, is the delicate yet crucial balance between accepting responsibility for our actions and compassionately interrogating the underlying beliefs that may be inadvertently making our journey far more arduous than it needs to be. It's about understanding that while accountability is vital, our internal narratives about ourselves and our experiences wield immense power, capable of either propelling us forward or holding us captive.

Understanding the Difference: Beliefs, Feelings, and "True Justified Belief" – A Friendly Chat

It's absolutely vital for this beautiful work of transformation to gently distinguish between your beliefs, your feelings, and objective truth. These three are often tangled together, creating a confusing internal landscape, aren't they?

- **Feelings:** Emotions are undeniably real experiences, my friend. When you feel sad, angry, joyful, or fearful, that emotional state is authentic to you in that moment. However, feelings are not always accurate barometers of objective truth or reliable guides for action. You can feel like a complete failure after a minor setback, but that feeling doesn't mean you are objectively a failure. Feelings are very often the product of our thoughts, and our thoughts, as we've seen, are powerfully generated and shaped by our underlying beliefs. So, a strong feeling might simply indicate a strongly held belief, not necessarily an external reality.

- **Beliefs:** As we've chatted about at length, beliefs are the convictions, the mental constructs, we hold to be true. They are our personal maps of reality. But critically, they are not necessarily objective facts; they are interpretations and conclusions drawn from our experiences. The statement, "I make decisions based on how I experience things, not the truth. They're not always the same," lovingly underscores this perfectly. Our beliefs are subjective lenses.

- **Truth (or True Justified Belief):** In the philosophical realm, particularly in epistemology (the theory of knowledge), a "True Justified Belief" is often considered a cornerstone of what constitutes knowledge. This means that for something to be genuinely known, it isn't enough to simply believe it, nor is it enough for it to happen to be true by chance. There must also be good reasons, sound evidence, or valid justification for holding that belief. In the context of our personal transformation, we are aiming to gently dismantle beliefs that are not true or are no longer justified (even if they once served a protective purpose) and systematically replace them with beliefs that are empowering, more closely aligned with objective reality (as best as we can ascertain it), and supported by conscious, reasoned choice, or by new, deliberately sought-after evidence.

Many of our most limiting beliefs, my dear friend, gently fail the "true justified belief" test. They are often old, inherited without scrutiny from family or culture, or based on hasty generalizations or misinterpretations of isolated past events. The emotional charge accompanying a belief can be incredibly potent, making the belief feel like an undeniable, unshakeable truth. This is where courage is required: to step back, to separate the intensity of the emotion from the factual validity of the belief itself, and to ask, "Just because I feel this strongly, does that make this belief objectively true and universally applicable?" My outrage over the "failure" headline was a strong feeling tied to an old belief about public perception. The truth, however, was that this perceived failure led to immense growth and learning. It was a brutal lesson, but a deeply valuable one.

THE ISLAND STRATEGIES

Actionable Strategies: Gently Rewriting Your Story

Reshaping your beliefs is not a passive exercise, my friend; it is an active, ongoing process of courageous self-discovery and intentional mental reprogramming. It's about consciously choosing the "software" that will lovingly run your life. And remember that empowering declaration: "Yes... you can change your belief to get where you want to go." This isn't just a hopeful platitude; it's a statement of your inherent capacity for mental and emotional evolution. As Henry Ford famously put it, "Whether you think you can, or you think you can't – you're right."

Here's a friendly, step-by-step guide to help you gently find, challenge, and lovingly transform those negative or limiting core beliefs:

1. Let's Identify the Belief: Become a Gentle Detective of Your Own Mind

This first step asks you to be a kind, honest detective of your own mind.

- **Listen Closely to Your Self-Talk:** What are those repetitive negative phrases, criticisms, or despairing statements that gently loop in your internal dialogue, especially when you're feeling stressed or facing a challenge? "I always...", "I never...", "I can't..." These are often soft clues to hidden beliefs.
- **Gently Examine Your "Shoulds," "Musts," and "Have Tos":** These words often signal underlying, rigid rules and beliefs about yourself and the world. "I should always put others

first." "I must be perfect to be accepted." Who decided you *should*?

- **Trace Back Your Biggest Fears:** What specific beliefs about your capabilities, your worth, or the nature of the world are gently fueling your most significant fears? Fear of failure might be rooted in the belief, "My worth depends on my achievements."
- **Look for Recurring Negative Patterns in Your Life:** Are there unwanted outcomes that seem to gently repeat in your relationships, career, or finances? What underlying beliefs might be unconsciously driving these patterns? For example, a pattern of attracting unreliable partners might stem from a belief like, "I'm not worthy of a committed, loving relationship."
- **Powerfully Complete the Sentence:** Take a current challenge or aspiration and gently complete the sentence: "I can't ___ (achieve this goal/make this change) because ___." The reason you give often directly reveals a core limiting belief.

2. Let's Challenge the Belief: Cross-Examine with Compassion

Once a limiting belief is gently brought into the light (e.g., "I'm not good enough to succeed in my own business," or "I'll always be overweight"), you must interrogate it relentlessly, like a skilled lawyer cross-examining an unreliable witness, but with so much compassion:

- **Origins Inquiry:** "Where did this belief actually come from? Can I pinpoint specific experiences, SEEs, or messages from others that led to its formation? Was it my own conclusion, or something I lovingly absorbed from someone else?" Digging into the past can gently reveal how flimsy some of these foundations are.
- **The 100% Truth Test:** "Is this belief 100% true, all the time, in

every single circumstance, without any exception whatsoever? Can I find even *one* instance in my own life, or in the lives of others, where this belief was not true?" (The answer is almost always no for broad limiting beliefs). If it's not 100% true, it's not a universal law; it's just *your* belief.
- **Evidence Audit:** "What concrete, objective evidence truly supports this belief? And, equally importantly, what evidence contradicts it or offers an alternative perspective? Am I selectively focusing on evidence that confirms my belief and ignoring evidence that challenges it (confirmation bias)?" Be a scientist about your truth, not just a believer.
- **Cost-Benefit Analysis:** "What are the real, tangible costs of holding onto this belief? How does it limit my actions, affect your happiness, damage your health, strain your relationships, or sabotage your goals? What do I gain by keeping it (e.g., a sense of safety, an excuse not to try)?" Is it really serving you, or just gently holding you back?
- **The Liberation Question:** "What would be the specific benefits of letting go of this belief? How would my life open up? What new possibilities would emerge?" Envision the beautiful freedom.
- **The Counterfactual Imagination:** "If this belief weren't true for me, what would I be doing differently right now? What would I dare to attempt? Who would I become?" Let your imagination gently show you the alternatives.
- **Positive Intention (Optional but helpful):** "Did this belief ever serve a positive or protective purpose for me in the past, even if it's no longer helpful? Can I acknowledge that past function without needing to keep the belief?" Sometimes beliefs served us well in childhood, but now they're holding us back like an old, outgrown coat.

3. Let's Transform the Belief: You're the Author Now!

This is where you actively and lovingly rewrite your script. You're the author of your own internal narrative now.

- **Formulate a new belief** that is positive, empowering, directly counters the old limiting belief, and is aligned with your desired reality and your highest potential.
    - **Old Limiting Belief Example:** "I'm not good enough to succeed in my own business."
    - **New Empowering Belief Example:** "I am inherently capable, resourceful, and committed to continuous learning. I possess unique strengths and perspectives that I can leverage to build a thriving and impactful business." OR "Every experience, whether perceived as a success or a setback, is a valuable learning opportunity that moves me closer to achieving my business goals and vision."
    - **Old Limiting Belief Example:** "I'll never find a loving partner."
    - **New Empowering Belief Example:** "I am worthy and capable of creating a deeply loving, supportive, and fulfilling partnership. I attract positive and healthy relationships into my life."

How to Gently Install and Truly Make Those New, Empowering Beliefs Stick

Identifying a new, empowering belief is a critical step, but it's only the beginning, my dear friend. To make it your new default operating system, you must actively install and consistently reinforce it until its neural pathways are stronger than those of the old, limiting belief.

- **Affirmations (Conscious Reprogramming):**
    - Craft concise, positive statements phrased in the present tense, as if your new belief is already an

established reality (e.g., "I am worthy of abundant love and success," "I attract financial prosperity with ease and joy," "I am a confident, articulate, and capable communicator," "I trust my intuition to guide me wisely").
  - Engage in the regular, dedicated repetition of these affirmations. Say them aloud with genuine feeling and conviction. Write them down repeatedly in a journal. Post them where you'll see them frequently (bathroom mirror, computer monitor, car dashboard). The key is consistency and emotional engagement. My mantra, "I will not go quietly into that good night. I will rage against the dying of the light," is more than just a powerful quote; it's a constant affirmation that reshapes my beliefs about resilience and determination, a defiant roar against anything that tries to hold me back.

- **Visualization (Mental Rehearsal for Reality):**
  - Devote regular time (even 5-10 minutes daily) to vividly visualize yourself living your life as if your new empowering belief is already fully integrated and true.
  - Imagine in detail how you would think, feel, speak, and act if this new belief were your unwavering reality. See yourself successfully navigating situations and achieving goals that were previously blocked or sabotaged by the old limiting belief. Engage all your senses in this mental movie: What do you see, hear, feel, even smell or taste in this new reality? The more vivid and emotionally resonant the visualization, the more powerfully it imprints on your subconscious. Your brain doesn't always know the difference between vividly imagined and real experiences.

- **Acting "As If" (Behavioral Congruence):**
  - This is about gently bridging the gap between belief and behavior. Consciously choose to behave in ways that are fully consistent with your new empowering belief, even if it feels uncomfortable, unfamiliar, or inauthentic at first. This is where courage meets action.
  - If your new belief is "I am a confident and engaging public speaker," then act "as if" you embody that confidence when you have an opportunity to speak (stand tall, make eye contact, use clear and expressive language, smile), even if your internal state is still one of nervousness. I often say, "If I can say to you that I am as confident running my business as I am running my children, you can say to me, 'You're pretty confident.'" It's because I've acted "as if" for so long that the confidence became real. When I play softball with my daughters, I may have to catch the ball with my right hand, tuck it under my arm, then pull it back down to throw, but I still hit the ball faster and harder than most. That's acting "as if" my unique physical makeup is a strength, not a limitation. Psychologically, this creates a form of cognitive dissonance that your mind will seek to resolve by aligning your internal state (belief) with your external actions. Action can indeed precede and then powerfully reshape both feeling and belief.

- **Gathering New Evidence (Building a Case for Your New Truth):**
  - Become a gentle detective for your new belief. Actively look for, acknowledge, and even celebrate any experiences, feedback, or observations, however small, that support and validate your new empowering belief. This consciously directs your brain's attentional filter

(the reticular activating system) to find proof that your new belief is true, thereby strengthening its neural pathways and diminishing the hold of the old one. Every little win is a piece of evidence.

- **Curate Your Environment (Supportive Influences):**
  - Spend more time with people who uplift you, who believe in your potential, and who reflect or embody the empowering beliefs you are cultivating. Seek out mentors, supportive friends, or communities that align with your growth.
  - Consciously limit your exposure to overly negative, critical, or cynical environments and individuals that might trigger old patterns of thought or reinforce the limiting beliefs you are working to release. Just like you wouldn't keep rotting food in your fridge, don't keep toxic influences in your life if you can help it.

- **Embrace Patience and Persistence (The Marathon Mindset):**
  - Reshaping deeply ingrained core beliefs, especially those formed in early life, is a marathon, not a sprint. It requires consistent effort, patience, and self-compassion. There will inevitably be moments when old beliefs resurface, particularly during times of stress or challenge.
  - When this happens, acknowledge their appearance without judgment or self-criticism. See them as old echoes, like a dusty old record playing a forgotten tune. Then, gently but firmly redirect your focus and energy back to your new, empowering beliefs and the practices that reinforce them. This is not a one-time fix or a magic bullet but a continuous, iterative process of upgrading

your internal operating system, one conscious choice at a time. My daughter Mackenzie, crying on the softball field wanting to quit, learned the lesson: "We don't quit on what we said we wanted to do." The next week, she got a base hit. This wasn't a magic fix; it was persistence and belief in herself. It was about showing up, even when it was hard, and trusting that the effort would pay off.

By diligently and courageously engaging in this process of reshaping your beliefs, you are fundamentally changing the very architecture of your perceived reality. You are systematically tearing down the invisible fences that have confined your potential and actively reprogramming your "Island of One" for limitless growth, profound resilience, and authentic thriving. This is the ultimate act of self-creation, the seventh and culminating key to unlocking the extraordinary life you were truly destined to live. It's about building the island of your dreams, brick by conscious brick.

CHAPTER IX: S is for Strengthen (Your Beliefs) Reshaping Your Beliefs

PART III

Action, Insight, and Transformation

CHAPTER X

Your COMPASS in Practice: The Scoring System and Validating Your Choices

"The COMPASS System empowers you to make fast, accurate, and aligned decisions, enabling you to confidently 'go left or right' on your unique life path."

We've now explored each of the seven powerful keys that make up your personal **C.O.M.P.A.S.S. System**. You understand the profound importance of Clarity, Ownership, Time Management, Perspective, Acknowledging Fears, Satisfying Needs, and Strengthening Beliefs. But how do you take these profound insights and translate them into a concrete, actionable process for navigating life's critical decisions? This chapter provides the practical playbook. We'll introduce the **C.O.M.P.A.S.S. Decision Cards**, a simple yet powerful scoring mechanism designed to help you quantify the alignment of your choices with your deepest purpose, and then guide you through essential "checks and

CHAPTER X: Your Compass in Practice

balances" to validate your decisions with unwavering confidence. This is where your blueprint comes to life.

The C.O.M.P.A.S.S. Decision-Making Methodology: A Scoring System

Inspired by direct, rapid assessment methods used in various successful systems, the **C.O.M.P.A.S.S. System** proposes a card-based scoring mechanism. This tool facilitates a quick "A or B" choice assessment against each of the seven keys, allowing users to tally a score that guides them towards the most aligned decision.

Concept: COMPASS Decision Cards

Imagine a deck of 7 specially designed cards, one for each letter of C.O.M.P.A.S.S. Each card offers prompts and questions tailored to its respective key, helping you evaluate a specific decision you're facing. While the core methodology can be applied mentally with a simple pen and paper, the most dynamic and powerful way to utilize the COMPASS System is through the interactive digital tool available at IslandofOne.com (which we'll discuss further later). Physical cards are also available for those who prefer a tactile experience.

How it Works (The Scoring Mechanism):

1. **Define the Decision:** Start by clearly identifying a specific "left or right" decision you need to make. This could be anything from a major life choice to a daily dilemma. For example:

    - "Should I take Job Offer A or Job Offer B?"
    - "Should I invest in Project X or Project Y?"
    - "Should I move to City A or City B?"
    - "Should I start my own freelance business or stay in my current stable corporate job?"

2. **The Two Options:** Clearly state the two choices being evaluated. Label them simply as "Choice A" and "Choice B."

3. **Iterate Through the 7 Keys:** For each of the seven COMPASS keys, you will systematically evaluate how *each* of your two choices (Choice A and Choice B) aligns with that key.

    o **Read the card's prompt and questions:** These are designed to make you consider your decision through the lens of that specific key.
    o **Select the "A", "B", or "C" option:** For each question on the card, choose the option that best reflects how Choice A aligns, and then separately, how Choice B aligns.
    o **Assign points:** Each "A", "B", or "C" response on the card will have an associated point value:

        - **A) Strong Alignment:** +2 points
        - **B) Moderate/Neutral Alignment:** 0 points
        - **C) Misalignment/Negative Impact:** -1 or -2 points *(depending on severity)*

4. **Tally the Score:** After going through all 7 COMPASS cards for *both* choices, sum up the total positive and negative points for "Choice A" and "Choice B" separately.

5. **Interpret the Results:** The choice with the higher overall positive score (or less negative score) indicates the decision most aligned with the principles of the COMPASS System and, by extension, your inherent design for thriving.

Example **COMPASS Card** Structure *(for a hypothetical "Job Offer A vs. Job Offer B" decision):*

Let's walk through an example. Meet Sarah, who is contemplating a significant career decision: "Should I start my own freelance

CHAPTER X: Your Compass in Practice

business (Choice A) or stay in my current stable corporate job (Choice B)?" We'll apply each COMPASS key to her scenario.

COMPASS Card: C - Clarity (Your Plan)

- **Prompt:** "Consider how each job offer aligns with your long-term vision and 'Thrive Plan'."

- **Questions for Choice A (Start Freelance Business):**

  o Does this job offer a clear path towards your ultimate career goals?
    A) Yes, it significantly accelerates my path. (+2)
    B) Not directly, but it's a step. (0)
    C) It diverges from my clear path. (-1)

  o Does this role clarify your purpose and light you up?
    A) Absolutely, it ignites my passion. (+2)
    B) Somewhat, but not entirely. (0)
    C) It feels misaligned with my core purpose. (-1)

- **Questions for Choice B (Stay in Current Corporate Job):**

  o Does this job offer a clear path towards your ultimate career goals?

    A) Yes, it significantly accelerates my path. (+2)
    B) Not directly, but it's a step. (0)
    C) It diverges from my clear path. (-1)

  o Does this role clarify your purpose and light you up?

    A) Absolutely, it ignites my passion. (+2)
    B) Somewhat, but not entirely. (0)
    C) It feels misaligned with my core purpose. (-1)

- **Hypothetical User's Choices & Scoring (Sarah):**

- **User's Perspective:** Sarah feels stagnant in her current corporate role (Choice B). She's been dreaming of having more creative control and making a direct impact, which aligns with her long-held "Thrive Plan" of building a legacy project.

  - **Choice A (Freelance Business):**
    - Q1: A) Yes, it significantly accelerates my path. (**+2 points**)
    - Q2: A) Absolutely, it ignites my passion. (**+2 points**)
    - *Sub-total for Choice A: +4 points*

  - **Choice B (Corporate Job):**
    - Q1: B) Not directly, but it's a step. (**0 points**)
    - Q2: C) It feels misaligned with my core purpose. (**-1 points**)
    - *Sub-total for Choice B: -1 point*

- **Analysis for This Key (Clarity):** For Sarah, the freelance business (Choice A) scores significantly higher on Clarity because it directly aligns with her long-term vision and ignites her passion, indicating a strong sense of purpose. Staying in the corporate job (Choice B), while familiar, feels like a detour from her true calling. This key strongly favors Choice A.

COMPASS Card: O - Ownership (Your Gifts)

- **Prompt:** "How does each choice allow you to leverage your unique innate gifts and the strengths forged from your past challenges?"

- **Questions for Choice A (Start Freelance Business):**

  - Does starting this freelance business allow you to fully utilize your core strengths (e.g., creativity, problem-solving, leadership)?

    A) Yes, it's a direct application of my strongest talents.

CHAPTER X: Your Compass in Practice

(+2)
B) Partially, some talents will be used. (0)
C) Not really, it feels outside my natural strengths. (-1)

- Does this choice leverage resilience or unique insights gained from past difficulties (e.g., adapting to change, financial setbacks, overcoming criticism)?

  A) Absolutely, past challenges have perfectly prepared me for this. (+2)
  B) It might, but it's not the primary focus. (0)
  C) It feels like it ignores or avoids lessons from my past. (-1)

- Will this path allow you to develop new skills that align with your natural aptitudes?

  A) Yes, significant and aligned skill growth is certain. (+1)
  B) Possibly, but it's not guaranteed. (0)
  C) No, it feels stagnant in terms of personal development. (-1)

- **Questions for Choice B (Stay in Current Corporate Job):**

  - Does staying in this job allow you to fully utilize your core strengths

    (e.g., creativity, problem-solving, leadership)?
    A) Yes, I consistently apply my best talents. (+1)
    B) Sometimes, but often I feel underutilized. (0)
    C) No, I feel my talents are stifled here. (-2)

  - Does this choice leverage resilience or unique insights gained from past difficulties?

    A) Yes, I can apply past lessons to current challenges. (+1)
    B) Only minimally; it doesn't challenge me much. (0)

C) It reinforces a comfort zone that avoids past lessons. (-1)

- Will this path allow you to develop new skills that align with your natural aptitudes?
  A) Yes, there are clear opportunities for aligned growth. (+1)
  B) Some minor development, but nothing significant. (0)
  C) No, I've plateaued in this role. (-1)

- **Hypothetical User's Choices & Scoring (Sarah):**

  - **User's Perspective:** Sarah is a highly creative problem-solver, a skill she honed during a challenging startup experience that ultimately failed. Her corporate job requires her to follow rigid processes, limiting her creativity.

  - **Choice A (Freelance Business):**
    - Q1: A) Yes, it's a direct application of my strongest talents. (**+2 points**)
    - Q2: A) Absolutely, past challenges have perfectly prepared me for this. (**+2 points**)
    - Q3: A) Yes, significant and aligned skill growth is certain. (**+1 point**)
    - *Sub-total for Choice A: +5 points*

  - **Choice B (Corporate Job):**
    - Q1: C) No, I feel my talents are stifled here. (**-2 points**)
    - Q2: B) Only minimally; it doesn't challenge me much. (**0 points**)
    - Q3: C) No, I've plateaued in this role. (**-1 point**)
    - *Sub-total for Choice B: -3 points*

- **Analysis for This Key (Ownership):** Sarah's freelance venture (Choice A) clearly aligns with her innate gifts and allows her

CHAPTER X: Your Compass in Practice

to leverage her hard-won resilience from past difficulties, promising significant growth. Her current corporate job (Choice B) actively stifles these talents, leading to a negative score. This key also strongly advocates for Choice A.

COMPASS Card: M - Manage (Your Time)

- **Prompt:** "How does each choice impact your ability to master your time, prioritize effectively, and maintain work-life balance?"

- **Questions for Choice A (Start Freelance Business):**

    o Will starting this business give you more control and flexibility over your schedule and time?

    A) Yes, I will design my ideal schedule. (+2)
    B) It will be demanding initially, but offers long-term flexibility. (0)
    C) No, I anticipate less control and more overwhelm. (-1)

    o Does this choice align with your long-term priorities for personal well-being and relationships?

    A) Absolutely, it supports my holistic life goals. (+2)
    B) It will require careful management to balance. (0)
    C) It feels like it will sacrifice my personal life. (-1)

    o Does this decision reduce or increase the "time robbers" (worry, want, procrastination, distractions) in your life?
    A) It empowers me to significantly reduce them. (+1)
    B) It might introduce new ones, but I'll manage. (0)
    C) It will dramatically increase them. (-1)

- **Questions for Choice B (Stay in Current Corporate Job):**

    o Does staying in this job allow you to maintain or improve control over your schedule and time?

A) Yes, my current schedule is predictable and manageable. (+1)
B) It's stable, but I have limited control or flexibility. (0)
C) No, my time is constantly dictated by others and feels overwhelming. (-2)

- Does this choice align with your long-term priorities for personal well-being and relationships?
  A) Yes, it provides stability for my personal life. (+1)
  B) It's adequate, but not ideal for my desired balance. (0)
  C) It consistently compromises my personal well-being and relationships. (-1)

- Does this decision reduce or increase the "time robbers" in your life?
  A) It helps maintain a predictable level of "noise." (+1)
  B) It has a consistent level of distractions. (0)
  C) It continually increases my worry and procrastination. (-1)

- **Hypothetical User's Choices & Scoring (Sarah):**
  - **User's Perspective:** Sarah's current corporate job has unpredictable hours and frequent urgent requests, leading to burnout. While freelance work has an initial learning curve, she envisions setting her own hours long-term.

  - Choice A (Freelance Business):
    - Q1: B) It will be demanding initially, but offers long-term flexibility. (**0 points**)
    - Q2: A) Absolutely, it supports my holistic life goals. (**+2 points**)
    - Q3: B) It might introduce new ones, but I'll manage. (**0 points**)
    - Sub-total for Choice A: +2 points

  - Choice B (Corporate Job):

CHAPTER X: Your Compass in Practice

- Q1: C) No, my time is constantly dictated by others and feels overwhelming. (**-2 points**)
- Q2: C) It consistently compromises my personal well-being and relationships. (**-1 point**)
- Q3: C) It continually increases my worry and procrastination. (**-1 point**)
- *Sub-total for Choice B: -4 points*

- **Analysis for This Key (Manage):** While Sarah acknowledges the initial time demands of starting a freelance business (Choice A), its long-term potential for control over her schedule and alignment with holistic life goals makes it score positively. The corporate job (Choice B) is a clear negative as it contributes to overwhelm and compromises her personal life. This key strongly points towards Choice A.

COMPASS Card: P - Perspective (Your Past)

- **Prompt:** "How does each choice allow you to reframe past setbacks into lessons and move beyond old patterns, rather than triggering old fears?"

- **Questions for Choice A (Start Freelance Business):**
  o Does starting this business allow you to apply hard-won lessons from past mistakes or challenges in a constructive way?

  A) Yes, it's a direct opportunity to implement past learnings. (+2)
  B) It might, but the connection isn't explicit. (0)
  C) It feels like it could repeat past negative patterns. (-1)

  o Does this choice empower you to challenge old narratives about your capabilities or limitations that might stem from past "failures" or criticisms?

  A) Absolutely, it's a powerful statement of moving forward. (+2)
  B) It's a new path, but doesn't directly address old

narratives. (0)
C) It triggers strong fears of repeating past disappointments. (-1)

- Will this decision help you shed the weight of past regrets or resentments, transforming them into fuel for growth?

    A) Yes, it offers a fresh start and a positive redirection of energy. (+1)
    B) It's neutral in terms of processing old emotions. (0)
    C) It might make me dwell on what went wrong before. (-1)

- **Questions for Choice B (Stay in Current Corporate Job):**
  - Does staying in this job allow you to apply hard-won lessons from past mistakes or challenges in a constructive way?

    A) Yes, I can apply lessons to improve my current situation. (+1)
    B) Only in a limited capacity within the existing structure. (0)
    C) It feels like I'm stuck in a loop, not learning new lessons. (-1)

  - Does this choice empower you to challenge old narratives about your capabilities or limitations?

    A) It offers opportunities for incremental growth within established boundaries. (+1)
    B) It maintains the status quo, neither challenging nor reinforcing old narratives. (0)
    C) It reinforces a perceived inability to break free from comfortable patterns. (-2)

  - Will this decision help you shed the weight of past regrets or resentments?

A) Yes, I'm content with my past choices here. (+1)
B) It's a stable choice, but doesn't actively resolve past internal conflicts. (0)
C) It keeps me in a situation that reminds me of past compromises. (-1)

- **Hypothetical User's Choices & Scoring (Sarah):**
  - **User's Perspective:** Sarah's earlier startup failure left her with a lot of self-doubt and a fear of risk. Her current job is "safe," but it constantly reminds her of her unfulfilled ambitions from the past.

  - **Choice A (Freelance Business):**
    - Q1: A) Yes, it's a direct opportunity to implement past learnings. (**+2 points**)
    - Q2: A) Absolutely, it's a powerful statement of moving forward. (**+2 points**)
    - Q3: A) Yes, it offers a fresh start and a positive redirection of energy. (**+1 point**)
    - *Sub-total for Choice A: +5 points*

  - **Choice B (Corporate Job):**
    - Q1: C) It feels like I'm stuck in a loop, not learning new lessons. (**-1 point**)
    - Q2: C) It reinforces a perceived inability to break free from comfortable patterns. (**-2 points**)
    - Q3: C) It keeps me in a situation that reminds me of past compromises. (**-1 point**)
    - *Sub-total for Choice B: -4 points*

- **Analysis for This Key (Perspective):** The freelance business (Choice A) presents a powerful opportunity for Sarah to actively reframe her past failure as a learning experience and overcome old narratives of limitation. Staying in her corporate job (Choice B) would keep her tethered to past regrets and unfulfilled potential, scoring very negatively. This key strongly supports Choice A.

COMPASS Card: A - Acknowledge (Your Fears)

- **Prompt:** "Does this decision require you to confront significant fears in a healthy way, representing a courageous step forward, or is it driven by avoidance?"

- **Questions for Choice A (Start Freelance Business):**
  - Does this choice directly involve confronting a major fear (e.g., fear of failure, financial insecurity, public judgment)?

    A) Yes, and I'm ready to lean into that growth. (+2)
    B) It has elements of fear, but I feel prepared. (+1)
    C) It feels overwhelmingly scary and potentially paralyzing. (-1)

  - Does this decision represent a courageous step outside your comfort zone, expanding your personal boundaries?

    A) Absolutely, it's a bold move for growth. (+2)
    B) Yes, it's a stretch, but manageable. (+1)
    C) No, it feels like a reckless leap rather than a courageous step. (-1)

  - Will this path help you "feed your faith and starve your fears" by fostering resilience and confidence?

    A) Yes, I believe it will build tremendous inner strength. (+1)
    B) It presents challenges that could test my resilience. (0)
    C) It could amplify my existing anxieties and doubts. (-1)

- **Questions for Choice B (Stay in Current Corporate Job):**
  - Does staying in this job involve confronting a major fear, or does it primarily offer a sense of security from fear?

    A) It allows me to address fears within a controlled

CHAPTER X: Your Compass in Practice

environment. (+1)
B) It provides comfort and avoids confronting new fears. (0)
C) It's driven by a fear of the unknown or of leaving security. (-2)

- Does this decision represent a courageous step outside your comfort zone, expanding your personal boundaries?

  A) Yes, I am actively seeking challenges within this role. (+1)
  B) It keeps me within my existing comfort zone. (0)
  C) No, it feels like I'm stagnating out of fear of change. (-1)

- Will this path help you "feed your faith and starve your fears" by fostering resilience and confidence?

  A) It provides a stable base to build confidence in other areas. (+1)
  B) It's a neutral choice; my confidence is stable. (0)
  C) It subtly reinforces a fear of taking risks or pursuing ambition. (-1)

- **Hypothetical User's Choices & Scoring (Sarah):**

  - **User's Perspective:** Sarah admits she's terrified of the financial insecurity of freelancing (fear of extinction, mutilation of financial well-being). However, she knows deep down that avoiding this challenge would lead to greater regret. She feels ready to confront this fear head-on.

  - **Choice A (Freelance Business):**
    - Q1: A) Yes, and I'm ready to lean into that growth. **(+2 points)**

- Q2: A) Absolutely, it's a bold move for growth. (**+2 points**)
- Q3: A) Yes, I believe it will build tremendous inner strength. (**+1 point**)
- *Sub-total for Choice A: +5 points*

  ○ **Choice B (Corporate Job):**
  - Q1: C) It's driven by a fear of the unknown or of leaving security. (**-2 points**)
  - Q2: C) No, it feels like I'm stagnating out of fear of change. (**-1 point**)
  - Q3: C) It subtly reinforces a fear of taking risks or pursuing ambition. (**-1 point**)
  - *Sub-total for Choice B: -4 points*

- **Analysis for This Key (Acknowledge):** Despite the significant fears associated with starting a business, Sarah's readiness to confront them and view it as a courageous, growth-oriented step makes Choice A score very high. Choice B, while offering comfort, is revealed as a path driven by avoidance of these fears, leading to a negative score. This key strongly supports Choice A as the path of courage.

COMPASS Card: S - Satisfy (Your Needs)

- **Prompt:** "Does this choice genuinely meet your core human needs (e.g., security, connection, growth, contribution) in a healthy way, or is it driven by a fleeting 'want'?"

- **Questions for Choice A (Start Freelance Business):**
  ○ Does this business genuinely meet your core needs for growth, autonomy, and potential contribution?

  A) Absolutely, it aligns perfectly with these deep needs. (**+2**)
  B) It meets some needs, but others might be challenged. (**0**)
  C) It's more of a superficial "want" than a deep need. (-

CHAPTER X: Your Compass in Practice

1)

- Will this decision provide healthy fulfillment without relying on unhealthy habits or temporary "sugar rushes"?

    A) Yes, it's a path to sustainable, intrinsic satisfaction. (+1)
    B) It has potential for both fulfillment and new stresses. (0)
    C) It might lead to seeking unhealthy coping mechanisms. (-1)

- Does this choice support your need for financial security and stability (even if it's a delayed gratification)?

    A) Yes, it's a calculated risk for long-term security. (+1)
    B) It introduces temporary financial uncertainty. (0)
    C) It feels financially reckless and jeopardizes security. (-1)

- **Questions for Choice B (Stay in Current Corporate Job):**

    - Does staying in this job genuinely meet your core needs for security, connection, or existing growth?

        A) Yes, it provides reliable fulfillment of these needs. (+1)
        B) It meets some needs, but others feel stagnant. (0)
        C) No, I feel unfulfilled and my core needs are unmet here. (-2)

    - Will this decision provide healthy fulfillment without relying on unhealthy habits or temporary "sugar rushes"?

        A) Yes, my current job provides consistent, healthy satisfaction. (+1)

B) It can lead to seeking external validation or escapism. (0)
C) I often feel the need to use unhealthy habits to cope. (-1)

- Does this choice support your need for financial security and stability?

  A) Yes, it offers strong and consistent financial security. (+2)
  B) It's financially stable, but I desire more. (0)
  C) While stable, it doesn't align with my financial aspirations for true abundance. (-1)

- **Hypothetical User's Choices & Scoring (Sarah):**

  - **User's Perspective:** Sarah feels her current job (Choice B) offers financial security but leaves her with an unmet need for growth and contribution. The freelance business (Choice A) offers higher growth and contribution potential, but with initial financial uncertainty. She values long-term growth and contribution deeply.

  - **Choice A (Freelance Business):**
    - Q1: A) Absolutely, it aligns perfectly with these deep needs. (**+2 points**)
    - Q2: A) Yes, it's a path to sustainable, intrinsic satisfaction. (**+1 point**)
    - Q3: B) It introduces temporary financial uncertainty. (**0 points**)
    - Sub-total for Choice A: +3 points

  - **Choice B (Corporate Job):**
    - Q1: C) No, I feel unfulfilled and my core needs are unmet here. (**-2 points**)

CHAPTER X: Your Compass in Practice

- Q2: B) It can lead to seeking external validation or escapism. (**0 points**)
- Q3: A) Yes, it offers strong and consistent financial security. (**+2 points**)
- *Sub-total for Choice B: 0 points*

- **Analysis for This Key (Satisfy):** Choice A (freelance) scores positively as it directly addresses Sarah's deep needs for growth and contribution, even with temporary financial trade-offs. Choice B (corporate) is neutral in terms of overall needs satisfaction, providing security but failing to meet other crucial needs, and even leading to unhealthy coping. This key also leans towards Choice A.

COMPASS Card: S - Strengthen (Your Beliefs)

- **Prompt:** "How does this decision strengthen an empowering belief about yourself, or does it reinforce a limiting one, aligning with the truth that you are 'built to thrive'?"

- **Questions for Choice A (Start Freelance Business):**

  o Does this choice reinforce the belief that you are capable of building something impactful and thriving on your own terms?

  A) Absolutely, it powerfully affirms my potential. (+2)
  B) It challenges my existing beliefs, which could be good. (+1)
  C) It triggers strong doubts about my self-worth and ability to succeed independently. (-1)

  o Does this decision align with the core truth that you are "built to thrive" and possess everything you need within?

  A) Yes, it's a testament to my inherent design for overcoming. (+2)
  B) It's a test of that belief, but I'm willing to try. (0)

C) It feels like I'm acting from a place of desperation or inadequacy. (-1)

o Will this path help you consistently apply affirmations and act "as if" you are successful, leading to a profound internal shift?

A) Yes, it's a perfect arena for daily belief reinforcement. (+1)
B) It requires significant effort to maintain a positive mindset. (0)
C) It will constantly challenge my ability to stay positive. (-1)

- **Questions for Choice B (Stay in Current Corporate Job):**

  o Does staying in this job reinforce the belief that you are capable of navigating your career successfully within an established structure?

  A) Yes, it affirms my competence in this environment. (+1)
  B) It maintains a neutral belief about my capabilities. (0)
  C) It reinforces a limiting belief that I can't succeed outside this role. (-2)

  o Does this decision align with the core truth that you are "built to thrive" and possess everything you need within?

  A) Yes, I can thrive and make an impact here. (+1)
  B) It doesn't actively push me to realize my full thriving potential. (0)
  C) It implicitly suggests I am not capable of thriving beyond this environment. (-1)

  o Will this path help you consistently apply affirmations and act "as if" you are successful, leading to a profound

CHAPTER X: Your Compass in Practice

internal shift?

A) Yes, I can reinforce empowering beliefs in this context. (+1)
B) It's stable, but doesn't actively inspire new belief work. (0)
C) It leads to self-talk about missed opportunities or stagnation. (-1)

- **Hypothetical User's Choices & Scoring (Sarah):**

  o **User's Perspective:** Sarah has a deep-seated limiting belief that she needs external validation and a "safe" structure to succeed. Starting her own business would directly challenge this, forcing her to rely on her inner strength. Staying in her job would reinforce the "safety" belief, hindering her growth.

  o **Choice A (Freelance Business):**

    - Q1: A) Absolutely, it powerfully affirms my potential. (**+2 points**)
    - Q2: A) Yes, it's a testament to my inherent design for overcoming. (**+2 points**)
    - Q3: A) Yes, it's a perfect arena for daily belief reinforcement. (**+1 point**)
    - *Sub-total for Choice A: +5 points*

  o **Choice B (Corporate Job):**

    - Q1: C) It triggers strong doubts about my self-worth and ability to succeed independently. (**-1 point**)
    - Q2: C) It implicitly suggests I am not capable of thriving beyond this environment. (**-1 point**)
    - Q3: C) It leads to self-talk about missed opportunities or stagnation. (**-1 point**)
    - *Sub-total for Choice B: -3 points*

- **Analysis for This Key (Strengthen):** Choice A (freelance) is a powerful catalyst for Sarah to strengthen empowering beliefs about her capabilities and inherent thriving nature. Choice B (corporate) reinforces limiting beliefs and self-doubt, leading to a highly negative score for this key. This key provides strong support for Choice A.

Overall Tally and Interpretation for Sarah's Scenario:

Let's sum up Sarah's scores for "Start Freelance Business (Choice A)" vs. "Stay in Corporate Job (Choice B)" across all 7 COMPASS keys:

COMPASS Key	Choice A (Freelance Business) Score	Choice B (Corporate Job) Score
C - Clarity	+4	-1
O - Ownership	+5	-3
M - Manage	+2	-4
P - Perspective	+5	-4
A - Acknowledge	+5	-4
S - Satisfy	+3	0
S - Strengthen	+5	-3
Total Score	**+29 points**	**-19 points**

Interpretation:

Based on the COMPASS scoring system, Choice A (starting her own freelance business) results in a significantly higher positive score

CHAPTER X: Your Compass in Practice

(+29) compared to Choice B (staying in her current corporate job) which yields a substantial negative score (-19).

Why This Is a Good Choice for Sarah (Based on Scores):

The scores across all seven COMPASS keys consistently and strongly indicate that starting the freelance business (Choice A) is the path most aligned with Sarah's personal growth, purpose, and long-term thriving.

- **Clarity & Ownership:** Choice A directly aligns with her purpose and passions, allowing her to fully utilize her creative problem-solving gifts, which are stifled in her current role.

- **Manage & Perspective:** While initially demanding, the freelance path promises long-term time mastery and provides a powerful opportunity to reframe past setbacks into valuable lessons, actively moving her beyond old patterns of self-doubt. Staying in the corporate job would perpetuate her feelings of being stuck and overwhelmed.

- **Acknowledge & Satisfy:** The freelance venture requires Sarah to courageously confront significant fears (like financial insecurity) in a healthy way, a crucial step for growth. It also addresses her deep needs for autonomy, growth, and contribution, which are unmet in her current job.
- **Strengthen:** Most importantly, Choice A directly challenges and helps to dismantle Sarah's limiting beliefs about her need for external structure and validation, powerfully affirming her capability to build something impactful on her own terms. Choice B would reinforce these limiting beliefs.

In essence, the COMPASS System guides Sarah towards the path that, while potentially more challenging in the short term, leads to profound personal alignment, fulfillment, and a stronger sense of being "built to thrive." The negative score for Choice B highlights that while it might offer temporary comfort, it is fundamentally misaligned with her core being and long-term aspirations.

Checks and Balances: Validating Your COMPASS Choice

The COMPASS System provides a powerful initial guide, helping you quantify the alignment of your choices with your inner blueprint. However, a wise captain never relies on a single instrument alone. To truly trust the decision the tool produces and to embark on your chosen path with maximum confidence, it's crucial to perform a series of "checks and balances" after completing the scoring. These steps leverage your intuition, external reality, and the wisdom of others, ensuring your chosen direction is robust and well-vetted.

1. The Intuition Check: Does It Resonate Deeply?

- **Method:** After tallying the scores and seeing the recommended choice, pause. Close your eyes. Take a few deep breaths. Now, ask yourself: "Does this outcome feel right in my gut? Does it resonate with my deepest inner knowing, even if there's still a hint of fear or uncertainty?"

- **Why it's important:** Your intuition is a powerful, often subconscious, aggregator of your experiences, values, and desires. As discussed in "Island of One," a life of intention means listening to your inner guidance. If the numerical result conflicts strongly with a persistent gut feeling, it's a signal to revisit the scoring or the underlying assumptions. This isn't about overriding logic, but integrating it with your intrinsic wisdom.
- **Example (Sarah):** Even though Choice A (freelance) was scary, when Sarah saw the strong positive score, she felt a profound sense of relief and excitement, a confirmation deep in her chest that this was the right direction, aligning perfectly with the "ping" her intuition had been giving her for months.

2. The Reality Check: Is It Feasible and Well-Informed?

- **Method:** Objectively assess the practical feasibility of the higher-scoring choice. This involves external research, gathering hard data, and potentially a small "pilot" or low-stakes test.

- ○ **Research:** What are the actual market conditions for a freelance business in your field? What are typical startup costs? What legal requirements exist?
- ○ **Small Pilot:** Can you take on a very small freelance project while still in your corporate job to test the waters, build a portfolio, or validate demand?
- ○ **Resource Assessment:** Do you have the necessary financial runway, skills (or a plan to acquire them), and network to support this choice?

- **Why it's important:** The COMPASS System helps align with your internal landscape, but decisions exist in the real world. This step ensures that your inspired choice is grounded in practicality and informed by current realities. It prevents dreams from becoming detached from execution, reinforcing the "Clarity (Your Plan)" and "Manage (Your Time)" keys.

- **Example (Sarah):** Sarah researched average freelance rates in her industry, identified potential initial clients, and even began saving a 9-month emergency fund. She also planned to take an online course on freelance business management while still employed, acting as a small pilot. This grounded her decision in reality, making it feel less like a reckless leap and more like a calculated, informed move.

3. The "Thrive Tribe" Consultation: Seeking Trusted Counsel

- **Method:** Share your two choices, your COMPASS scores, and your personal reflections with 1-3 trusted individuals from your "Thrive Tribe" - mentors, close friends, or family members who genuinely support your growth and offer honest, constructive feedback. Ask them for their objective insights, potential blind spots, and what they see as your strengths and challenges relating to each option.

- **Why it's important:** As "Island of One" emphasizes, connection is key. External perspectives can reveal valuable insights you might have missed. Your "Thrive Tribe" can act as a sounding board, offer alternative viewpoints, and provide accountability and encouragement. This step strengthens the "Love and Belonging" aspect of "Satisfy (Your Needs)" and supports a broader "Perspective."

- **Example (Sarah):** Sarah discussed her scores with a mentor who had successfully transitioned to freelancing and her best friend. Her mentor affirmed the alignment with her gifts and purpose, offering practical advice on managing initial financial dips. Her friend, knowing Sarah's tendencies, highlighted the importance of setting boundaries to prevent client overwhelm, a critical point for the "Manage (Your Time)" key.

4. The "Worst-Case Scenario" Playbook: Mitigating Potential Downsides

- **Method:** For the higher-scoring choice, actively envision the worst-case scenario that could realistically occur. What would be the biggest challenge or setback? Then, critically, brainstorm concrete steps you would take to address or mitigate that worst-case outcome. This isn't about dwelling on negativity, but about preparedness.

- **Why it's important:** This step directly engages with and helps to "Acknowledge (Your Fears)" in a constructive way. By having a plan for potential difficulties, you reduce the paralyzing power of fear and build confidence in your ability to adapt and overcome, reinforcing your inherent resilience. It transforms assumed future fears into actionable strategies.

- **Example (Sarah):** Sarah identified her worst fear as financial failure within six months and having to return to corporate. Her mitigation plan included: having a 9-month emergency fund, a list of previous corporate contacts for potential contract work if needed, and a clear "cut-off" date for reassessment if revenue targets weren't met. This proactive planning helped her feel more in control and less intimidated by the perceived risk.

5. The "Future Self" Reflection: Long-Term Alignment

- **Method:** Fast-forward yourself mentally to 1 year, 5 years, and 10 years in the future. Standing there, looking back at the decision you are about to make, how does your future self feel about this choice? Does it still feel like the right move, one that led to growth, fulfillment, and a life truly "built to thrive"?

- **Why it's important:** This exercise reinforces "Clarity (Your Plan)" and "Strengthen (Your Beliefs)" by connecting the present decision to your desired long-term identity and legacy. It helps ensure that short-term comfort or immediate desires don't derail your ultimate vision, and that the decision truly reflects who you aspire to become.

- **Example (Sarah):** Sarah imagined herself 5 years from now, having successfully built her freelance business. She saw herself with more freedom, creative fulfillment, and a profound sense of accomplishment, far more vibrant than her future self remaining in the corporate job. This powerful visualization solidified her conviction and resolve.

By incorporating these checks and balances, the **C.O.M.P.A.S.S. System** evolves beyond a simple scoring tool. It becomes a comprehensive, iterative decision-making process that integrates internal wisdom, external realities, and a proactive approach to potential challenges, allowing users to move forward with profound confidence and conviction.

This hands-on application of the **COMPASS System** is what transforms theoretical understanding into practical power, setting the stage for you to confidently navigate your unique life path.

CHAPTER XI
Action, Insight, and Transformation

" I'm comfortable almost being uncomfortable."

We've truly journeyed so far together, haven't we? We've gently peeled back so many layers, exploring those seven beautiful keys that unlock your incredible potential: discovering your unique Gifts, finding your rhythm with Time, lovingly reclaiming your Past, bravely charting your Plan, deeply honoring your Needs, tenderly befriending your Fears, and consciously reshaping your Beliefs. By now, I imagine you're seeing things with fresh eyes, feeling a much deeper understanding of what truly makes your heart sing, and perhaps even holding a gentle blueprint for building that life you've been dreaming of on your "Island of One."

But here's a little secret, and it's a big one, whispered just between us: all that amazing insight? All that profound understanding? It's like holding the most detailed, beautifully drawn map to buried treasure, but never quite picking up the shovel. It won't get you there, will it? This chapter, and really, this entire final part of our conversation, is all about the magic—the quiet alchemy—of actually *doing* the thing. It's about gently bridging that often-wobbly gap between knowing exactly what your heart yearns to do and, well, actually doing it. It's about transforming all that profound understanding into something tangible, something that truly, beautifully shifts your life.

Bridging the Gap: Those Tricky Places Between Knowing and Doing

Have you ever noticed, my dear friend, how many of us—and oh, myself included, more times than I care to admit—attend these incredible workshops, devour inspiring books, or have those "aha!" moments of crystal-clear clarity where you just *get* what needs to change in your life? You feel invigorated, inspired, ready to embrace the whole world! And then... days, weeks, maybe even months later, you find yourself quietly slipping back into the same old patterns. Feeling a little frustrated, a bit deflated, wondering why that initial spark didn't ignite a lasting flame.

It reminds me of something I've heard spiritual guides say, and it resonates so deeply: "You come to a sacred space on Sunday. You receive an amazing message. You feel truly good... And by Monday morning, you're back in the daily grind, maybe feeling those frustrations creep back in." That feeling of a powerful insight just... gently fading away in the relentless face of daily life? It's far too common, isn't it? It's like hitting a wall, and sometimes, that wall feels completely invisible until you gently bump right into it.

So, why does this sometimes maddening gap exist? Why do our very best intentions often quietly unravel? I've seen it, and I've lived it, truly. Here are some of the gentle, sneaky pitfalls that love to derail our well-meaning plans:

- **Fear of Failure (or even Success):** Oh, this one is such a

CHAPTER XI: Action, Insight, and Transformation

classic, isn't it? Even with newfound understanding, those old fears (remember our chat in Key #6?) have a persistent way of resurfacing. They whisper doubts and anxieties, not just about stumbling, but sometimes, ironically, about what might happen if you actually succeed. What if things change too much? What if you can't quite handle the new amazingness?

I've certainly faced this. When I decided to launch my company, Insider Success, and then several other ventures, the fear was palpable. It wasn't just a mild discomfort; it was a tight knot in my stomach, a relentless drumbeat of "what ifs" in my head. Especially after the searing sting of past financial setbacks, including two business bankruptcies. Yes, you heard that right – two. There were days I felt smaller than an enigma, completely exposed and diminished. The memory of those past failures could have easily, should have, paralyzed me. There was no guarantee of success this time either, but this deep, gnawing necessity to act, to build something meaningful, to try again propelled me forward. It was a terrifying leap of faith, but staying put felt even worse.

- **Overwhelm:** Sometimes, the sheer number of beautiful changes we want to invite, or the sheer size of our audacious goals, just feels so... immense. It's like standing at the base of a magnificent mountain with no idea which way is up. We don't know where to gently begin, so we don't start at all. It's like trying to embrace an entire forest in one hug. You just stand there, frozen for a moment.

- **Lack of Clarity on First Steps:** While the grand vision, the overall plan, might sparkle clearly in your heart, the very next tangible, tiny action might feel a little hazy. And that lack of a clear starting point often gently leads straight to procrastination. We wait for inspiration, when often, action creates the inspiration, doesn't it?

- **Perfectionism:** Ah, the quiet whisper that can derail progress. The tender desire to do things perfectly can, ironically, prevent us from doing anything at all. We tell ourselves we're waiting for the "perfect" time, the "perfect" conditions, or the "perfect" plan. The beautiful truth? None of those ever fully arrive. And while we're gently waiting, life—and wonderful opportunities—can quietly pass us by.

- **Old Habits and Comfort Zones:** Our existing patterns of behavior are incredibly deeply ingrained, aren't they? They're like well-worn, familiar paths in the forest of our minds, and even if they lead us nowhere truly fulfilling, they offer a strange sense of familiarity and comfort. Stepping onto a new path, into new behaviors, lovingly demands conscious effort and, at first, feels incredibly new and sometimes a little uncomfortable. It's unfamiliar territory.

My good friend Chip Yates, that astonishing, record-breaking inventor who holds 18 Guinness World Records for the fastest electric airplane and motorcycle, spoke so eloquently about this. He said, "I'm comfortable almost being uncomfortable." Think about that for a second. Chip, who's worked for NASA and is this incredibly accomplished entrepreneur and patent holder, willingly embraces the discomfort of trying new things, even when it means breaking bones or blowing up battery packs (yes, literally!). His willingness to push boundaries, often to the point of physical discomfort and financial risk, is a powerful testament to this mindset. He understands that growth lives outside the comfort zone.

- **Lack of Sustained Motivation:** That initial burst of enthusiasm? It's amazing, but it can—and often does—gently wane. Without some kind of system, a tender nudge to keep the momentum going, it's all too easy to quietly slip back into old ways. The novelty wears off, and the daily rhythm sets in.

- **Forgetting the "Why":** We sometimes get so caught up in the "how" or the "what" that we lose touch with the deep, emotional reasons why we wanted to change in the first place. When you forget that powerful "why," the gentle drive to act diminishes, and the uphill climb can feel impossible.

- **External Resistance or Lack of Support:** Sometimes, it's not just us, is it? The world around us, or even the people closest to us, may not always be supportive of our beautiful changes. It gently creates extra hurdles, making an already tender journey even tougher.

  My formidable friend, Bill Mitchell, a former NFL player for the New York Giants and a dear friend and groomsman at my wedding, faced this head-on. Imagine his dream of playing professional football, and his own family didn't initially support it. Especially as a new father balancing college and a baby girl. He had to dig deep, find his own internal drive, and figure out external solutions just to pursue that audacious goal. The naysayers were loud, but his inner conviction was louder.

Recognizing these gentle pitfalls is more than half the battle, my friend. It's the first crucial step to lovingly navigating them. Because ultimately, action is the sturdy bridge across this gap. It's the only way we gently get from "I know" to "I am."

The Beautiful Power of Consistent Small Steps: Building Momentum Through Daily Empowering Habits and Routines

The very idea of transforming your entire life can feel like trying to move a mountain with a tiny spoon. It's overwhelming, right? But here's the beautiful, liberating secret: monumental change rarely happens in one gigantic leap. It's the quiet, often unglamorous, result of consistent, small, deliberate actions taken over time. Think of it like water gently carving through rock—not with one massive, forceful gush, but through persistent, steady application, drop by patient drop.

- **Habits as Autopilots for Success:** When you intentionally cultivate empowering daily habits – maybe a morning mindfulness practice, a peaceful evening review of your goals, squeezing in a quick workout, or dedicating time to learning something new – these behaviors eventually become automatic. They move from "things you have to remember to do" to simply "things you do." They become part of your island's natural, supportive rhythm, lovingly requiring less conscious effort and willpower.

    An old buddy of mine, Josh, is an incredible example of this. He overcame unimaginable odds, including living homeless out of a 1996 Honda Civic as a teenager. Think about that desperation, that fear, that feeling of having nothing. Yet, he transformed his life to become a highly successful Chief Marketing Officer and entrepreneur. Josh deeply emphasized the power of routine. He told me that his consistent morning meditation practice and intentional approach to each day were absolutely critical in his transformation from feeling like an imposter to embodying genuine success. It wasn't about one big break; it was about the disciplined comfort of a daily

CHAPTER XI: Action, Insight, and Transformation

rhythm that allowed him to rebuild himself.

- **Momentum is Your Ally:** Action, even tiny action, creates momentum. Even the smallest step forward gently generates a sense of accomplishment, a little spark of energy that makes the next step feel a little bit easier. Newton's first law of motion applies beautifully to personal change: an object in motion stays in motion. The hardest part, almost always, is just getting started. But once you do, even a little bit, the universe seems to conspire to help you keep going.

- **The Compound Effect:** This is where the real magic happens, my friend. Small, seemingly insignificant positive actions, when repeated consistently, compound over time to produce truly remarkable results. Saving a small amount of money each day, reading for just 15 minutes daily, or making one healthy food choice at each meal might not seem like much in isolation. But over weeks, months, and years, the cumulative impact is nothing short of transformative. It's like planting a tiny seed every day and then one day realizing you've lovingly grown a forest.

An old friend and guest on my old TV show that was on Amazon Prime years ago, "Life Can Change," Angelo Lombardo, a Fortune 50 executive, lived through a crisis that truly tested this. His infant daughter was born with a life-threatening congenital heart defect, a profound tragedy that brought him and his wife to their knees. Yet, Angelo, with remarkable courage, found a "gift" within it. And he firmly believes that "change, real change, real success in life comes from a lot of real tiny little things done well, and done consistently." His family's journey is a powerful, heartbreaking, yet ultimately hopeful testament to the cumulative strength of those small, persistent efforts, especially when the stakes are unbelievably high.

Please, my friend, don't ever underestimate the profound power of seemingly minor adjustments made consistently. If life seems routine, and that routine is built on disempowering habits, the outcome is predictable stagnation. But if you consciously design a routine built on small, empowering actions aligned with your "Thrive Plan," the outcome is predictable growth. It's your loving choice to design that routine, piece by consistent piece.

My Entrepreneurial Journey: A Story of Taking Action Despite Uncertainty and Perceived Limitations

My own path, especially in business, has been a messy, exhilarating, often terrifying testament to the absolute necessity of action. And more often than not, it's been action taken squarely in the face of profound uncertainty and what most people would see as significant limitations. When I first started my companies, particularly after experiencing the searing sting of bankruptcy (yes, again, it still feels raw to say it), the fear wasn't a gentle whisper; it was a roaring lion. The "what ifs" were loud, so loud they drowned out everything else. The memory of past failure (that old familiar friend from Key #3) could have easily, easily, paralyzed me. There was no shimmering guarantee of success, but this deep, undeniable necessity to act, to build something meaningful, to claw my way forward, just... propelled me.

- **Taking Calculated Risks**: Starting my conference center, as I've shared before, felt like a gargantuan risk. I remember thinking, "I'm fine running my companies... I don't need to speak to anybody... I've taken a building and turned it into an intimate center for change. What a risk that is." The internal debate was fierce. But here's the thing: it wasn't a reckless

CHAPTER XI: Action, Insight, and Transformation

gamble. It was a risk aligned with my deepest purpose (remember Key #1 – my gift for teaching, Key #5 – my need for contribution and significance). The action was a deliberate step, born from a vision I couldn't shake.

And then, even when my company faced a major setback – losing the ability to process credit card payments for several weeks (imagine that, in today's world!) – it forced me to truly re-evaluate. It was a gut check. Was my business really aligned with my core? Was the mission strong enough to push through this kind of chaos? It was a brutal test of resilience, and thankfully, it affirmed that the mission did matter enough. So I pushed.

- Problem-Solving in Action: When I was confronted with the challenge of flying an airplane with one hand, I didn't just accept the limitation. That wasn't in my nature. I took action, yes, but not in the way you might expect. First, I tried all these external devices, pouring thousands of dollars out of my own pocket into various prosthetics and contraptions for everyday tasks like lifting weights, swimming, or playing golf. Each device, each expenditure, felt like a tangible manifestation of a financial setback, a constant, nagging reminder of what I perceived as a physical lack.

But this prolonged, costly search for external fixes ultimately led to a far more valuable and liberating realization: the empowering truth that "God already gave me everything that I need." That pivotal understanding wasn't just a comforting spiritual notion; it became the critical setup for a more authentic, resourceful, and internally driven way of living. It prompted a profound shift from relying on cumbersome and expensive external crutches to discovering and trusting the inherent capabilities, the innate ingenuity, that resided within me all along. The true "device" was my own inherent adaptability, my own stubborn determination. My action wasn't just physical; it was a complete rethinking, a re-engineering of my approach to life itself.

- **Consistency Over Perfection:** Building my businesses, or frankly, building any meaningful life, wasn't about one brilliant, heroic move that changed everything overnight. Not for me, and probably not for you either. It was about showing up day after day. It was about making those dreaded phone calls, solving a new problem that popped up (and believe me, they always pop up), learning from countless mistakes, and persistently, stubbornly, moving forward, even when progress felt agonizingly slow, or setbacks felt like gut punches. It's the daily grind, the consistent application of effort, that builds enduring success. It's about getting back up, sometimes bruised, sometimes tired, but always choosing to take that next step.

The point of sharing all this isn't that I'm fearless, or that I always knew the outcome. Far from it. The point is that action was taken despite the fear, despite the uncertainty, despite the perceived limitations. Each step, each decision to act, built upon the last, creating the reality I now inhabit. Your journey will be unique, absolutely. But the principle of action remains universal. As the legendary Pablo Picasso wisely stated, *"Action is the foundational key to all success."* And it's a key you hold right now.

CHAPTER XI: Action, Insight, and Transformation

Actionable Strategies: Gently Igniting and Sustaining Your Transformation

Knowing is not enough; we must apply. Willing is not enough; we must do. So, let's talk about how to really translate all that amazing insight you've gained into consistent, transformative action. This is where the rubber meets the road, where the map turns into beautiful footsteps.

Creating a "Daily Thrive Ritual"

Think of your "Daily Thrive Ritual" as your personal power-up sequence for each day, my friend. It's a set of intentional practices you commit to each morning and evening to align yourself with your goals, nurture your well-being, and keep that beautiful momentum going. This isn't about piling on more overwhelming tasks; it's about strategically incorporating small, high-impact actions that truly fuel you.

- **Morning Anchor (Setting the Tone):**
  - **Mindful Wake-up:** Resist that immediate urge to grab your phone. Seriously, fight it. Instead, take a few precious moments for genuine gratitude or just quiet reflection. As I learned from Josh Roche, that remarkable entrepreneur I mentioned, getting up before others and practicing meditation was absolutely fundamental for him to gain control over his internal state and set the day's intention, especially after overcoming immense personal adversity. That quiet time before the world demands your attention is gold.

  - **Hydration & Movement:** First thing, drink a big glass of water. Then, engage in some light stretching, a short walk, or even just a quick 10-minute workout. I make it a point to never miss my morning ride, walk, or workout, even if it's just 20 minutes, because it's my sacred time. It's where I connect with myself, where ideas flow, and where I prime my body and mind for the day.

- **Review Your "Why" and Plan:** Briefly connect with your mission statement and the top 1-3 priorities from your "Thrive Plan" for the day. Remind yourself why you're doing what you're doing.

- **Affirmations/Visualization (Key #7):** Spend a moment reinforcing your empowering beliefs. See yourself achieving your goals, feel the emotions of success. This isn't just wishful thinking; it's actively programming your mind for success.

- **Midday Check-in (Maintaining Focus - Optional):**
  - A brief pause to assess progress, reset intentions, and practice a moment of mindfulness. Maybe a quick walk, a few deep breaths, or just stepping away from your screen for five minutes.

- **Evening Reflection & Preparation (Winding Down with Purpose):**
  - **Acknowledge Wins:** Before bed, take a moment to reflect. What went well today? What small steps did you take, no matter how tiny? Celebrate them!

  - **Lessons Learned:** What challenges popped up? What can you learn from them? This isn't about self-criticism, but objective learning.

  - **Plan for Tomorrow:** Briefly outline your top priorities for the next day. This creates clarity, reduces that morning decision fatigue, and sets you up for success.

- **Gratitude Practice:** End the day by focusing on what you're genuinely thankful for. It's a powerful way to shift your mindset before sleep.

- **Wind-Down Routine:** Disengage from screens at least an hour before bed. Read a physical book, meditate, listen to calming music, or engage in something else that helps you relax and prepare for restful sleep (Key #2). I've found that simply turning off the television and consciously creating silence is one of the most impactful steps anyone can take to change their life. Why? Because it allows for true focus, true self-connection, and space for your own thoughts to emerge, rather than being constantly bombarded by external noise.

Your ritual should be deeply personal, my dear friend. Start small—even just 15-20 minutes in the morning—and make it enjoyable. Consistency is far more important than length or perfection. It's about showing up for yourself, every single day.

Overcoming Inertia and the Gentle Resistance to Change

Inertia—that stubborn tendency to remain exactly where we are—is a powerful force, isn't it? And resistance to change? Totally natural. Our brains are hardwired for efficiency and familiarity, even if familiarity means staying stuck.

- **Identify Your Resistance Triggers:** What situations, thoughts, or feelings typically cause you to slam on the brakes when you know you need to take action? (Often, you'll find these are linked to old fears or limiting beliefs we talked about).

Get curious about them, rather than judging them.

- **Acknowledge and Validate the Resistance (Don't Fight It Directly):** This is key. Instead of beating yourself up for feeling resistant, just acknowledge it, gently: "Okay, I'm feeling really resistant to making those sales calls right now." Or "Wow, I'm really dragging my feet on this project." It's okay. Your brain just prefers the path of least resistance, like a river looking for the easiest way downhill. Don't fight the feeling; just observe it.

- **Connect to Your "Why":** Immediately remind yourself of the larger purpose, the compelling vision, or the deep benefit of taking that action. "Making these calls is a step towards building my business and achieving financial freedom, which means I can provide more for my family." Or "Finishing this project means I'm closer to that promotion that will give me more flexibility."

- **Break It Down (The "Swiss Cheese" Method):** If a task feels overwhelmingly enormous, break it into the smallest possible steps. Imagine you have a giant block of Swiss cheese, and you're just going to poke a tiny hole in it. What's one microscopic piece you can do right now? If writing a chapter feels too big, can you just write one single paragraph? Or even just outline the main points for 10 minutes? The goal is just to start, to create a little momentum.

- **Focus on the Process, Not Just the Outcome:** Sometimes, focusing too much on the big, daunting end result can be incredibly intimidating. Instead, shift your focus to consistently engaging in the process itself. Trust that if you faithfully execute the process, the outcome will follow. For example, instead of "I need to run a marathon," focus on "I will run for 20 minutes today, no matter what."

The 5-Second Rule and Other "Get Started" Techniques

The absolute hardest part, more often than not, is simply initiating action. These techniques are like little mental hacks that can help you override that hesitation and just go:

- **The 5-Second Rule (popularized by Mel Robbins):** This one is pure genius in its simplicity. When you have an instinct to act on a goal, but you feel yourself hesitating, count "5-4-3-2-1-GO" and literally, physically move. The counting interrupts that ingrained habit of hesitation and self-doubt, creating a tiny, precious window for action before your brain talks you out of it. It's like launching a rocket—once that countdown starts, there's no turning back!

- **The 2-Minute Rule (from David Allen's "Getting Things Done"):** If a task takes less than two minutes to complete, do it immediately instead of putting it on a to-do list. This clears small items quickly, reduces mental clutter, and gives you a satisfying sense of accomplishment right off the bat. Think: sending that quick email, washing that one dish, or putting away that stray item.

- **The "Just Five Minutes" Technique:** Tell yourself you'll only work on a dreaded task for five minutes. Set a timer. Often, once you start, you'll find that initial resistance melts away, and you'll find the motivation to continue for much longer. Getting over that initial hurdle is the key. You just need to trick yourself into starting.

- **Set a "Starting Line" Ritual:** Create a small, consistent ritual that signals the beginning of a work session or a particular task. Maybe it's clearing your desk, putting on specific music, making a cup of tea, or even just taking three deep breaths. This simple act can help transition your mind into action mode, telling your brain, "Okay, we're switching gears now; it's time to focus."

The journey from insight to transformation is truly paved with deliberate, consistent action, my friend. It's about choosing, day by day, moment by moment, to engage with your life actively rather than passively. It's about understanding that "Life can change if you make different choices," and then having the courage and the practical systems in place to make those choices consistently. The alchemy happens not in the grand pronouncements or the huge leaps, but in the quiet, persistent dedication to the small steps that, compounded over time, slowly but surely reshape your reality and bring your "Island of One" into its fullest, most vibrant expression.

As the ancient philosopher Lao Tzu sagely advised, "The journey of a thousand miles begins with a single step." Take yours. Today.

CHAPTER XII: How to Bounce Forward, Not Just Back

CHAPTER XII

How to Bounce Forward, Not Just Back

Here's another one of my core beliefs, one I often tell myself and others: "You must have Short Term Memory in order to make the next play." And trust me, this wisdom applies far beyond the football field.

The Resilience Engine: How to Bounce Forward, Not Just Back

Life on your "Island of One" isn't about navigating perpetually calm seas or somehow avoiding storms altogether. Honestly, that's an unrealistic expectation for any meaningful voyage. If you're truly living, you're going to hit rough patches. Instead, the real art of thriving lies in building a vessel so remarkably sturdy, an inner resilience so profoundly ingrained, that you not only weather the inevitable tempests but learn to skillfully harness their raw, formidable energy to propel you forward with even greater momentum and clarity.

I'm not just talking about bouncing *back* to where you were before. Oh no, we're aiming higher. We're talking about bouncing *forward*, emerging from each setback, each crushing challenge, not just intact, but demonstrably stronger, wiser, and more keenly aware of your own incredible capabilities. This, my friend, is the very essence of transformative resilience. As Epictetus, the ancient Stoic philosopher, so profoundly stated, "It's not what happens to you, but how you react to it that matters." And your reaction? That's where your power truly lies.

Feedback, Not Indictment
The Art of Learning from Life's Detours

The word "failure" itself... just hearing it can bring an undeniable, often crushing, weight, can't it? From the time we're little kids, we're subtly and overtly conditioned to see it as a definitive full stop, a final, damning judgment on our intrinsic worth or our capacity to achieve anything. It becomes this brand, this label we desperately fear, a ghost that haunts our biggest aspirations.

But what if we dared to strip "failure" of all that terrifying power? What if we radically reframed it, not as a harsh verdict, but as vital, unvarnished *feedback*? Imagine, as I've painfully learned through the crucible of my own two business bankruptcies—experiences where I "felt as if I was smaller than an enigma," utterly exposed and diminished, like my entire identity was crumbling—that what we call failure is simply life's unceremonious, yet profoundly instructive, way of saying: "Hey, this particular approach, this specific strategy, isn't yielding the desired result. It's time to gather the data, learn the hard lesson, and intelligently pivot. Try something else." It's like your personal GPS recalculating your route after a wrong turn—it doesn't judge you, it just calmly finds a new way forward.

Viewed through this lens, every "failure," every misstep, every unexpected setback transforms from a source of soul-crushing shame into an invaluable data point. It becomes a rich, fertile opportunity to learn, to recalibrate your compass, to adjust your sails, and to meticulously refine your plan of action.

When I embarked on the seemingly impossible journey of learning to type proficiently with one hand, or the intricate dance of figuring out how to coax melodies from a guitar, my path was absolutely *littered* with countless moments that, by conventional standards, could have been easily labeled "failures." Each misspelled word that stubbornly appeared on the screen, each awkward, buzzing chord that made my teeth hurt, each fumbled keystroke that broke the rhythm—these weren't declarations of my inadequacy. No. Instead, they were precise, practical lessons. They were clear signposts guiding me, step by painstaking step, toward innovation, toward creating my own unique methods.

The crucial insight here is this: you absolutely *must* decouple your intrinsic self-worth from the fluctuating outcomes of your endeavors. You are not defined by your failures, nor are you solely defined by your successes. These are merely events, experiences along the complex, winding road of your journey. They provide critical, actionable information for your next strategic move, your next courageous attempt.

And please, remember this: your failure to take a risk on what you *know* is the right path can keep old, unwanted patterns repeating themselves. The act of *avoiding* "failure" by systematically shying away from necessary risks, from stepping into the scary unknown, is the surest and most direct path to a life of stagnation, unfulfilled potential, and quiet regret. True growth blossoms in the rich soil of experimentation, and experimentation inherently involves the very real possibility of not getting it right the first time.

My friend Chip Yates, my incredibly accomplished friend and guest on "Life Can Change," with his 18 world records in electric vehicles, embodies this philosophy. He candidly shared that his path was "fraught with failures," including spectacular motorcycle crashes and terrifying moments where batteries blew up in his experimental electric airplane. Yet, he views these setbacks as "golden eggs"—precious opportunities to learn, adapt, and ultimately, to achieve even greater triumphs. His resilience is a testament to embracing, rather than frantically avoiding, the vital lessons hidden in every single fall. That's the mindset we're cultivating.

Embracing Challenges as Stepping Stones

Resilience, that powerful engine that drives us forward, isn't forged in a vacuum. It's deeply and inextricably intertwined with what Stanford psychologist Dr. Carol Dweck identifies as a "growth mindset." This is the profound, empowering belief that your abilities, your intelligence, and your talents are *not* fixed, immutable traits carved in stone at birth. Oh no. They are dynamic qualities that can be cultivated, developed, and significantly enhanced through unwavering dedication, persistent effort, and a deep commitment to lifelong learning. This perspective stands in stark contrast to a "fixed mindset," which operates from the incredibly limiting assumption that your qualities are largely static, that you either "have it" or you "don't," leaving very little room for meaningful change or development.

At the very heart of a growth mindset lies the active, even eager, embracing of challenges. Instead of viewing difficult tasks or unfamiliar situations as terrifying threats to your ego or potential harbingers of failure, you see them as invaluable opportunities to stretch your current boundaries, to acquire new skills, and to expand your capabilities in truly meaningful ways. Obstacles, from this powerful vantage point, cease to be demoralizing dead ends; they transform into intriguing puzzles, complex problems inviting your ingenuity and perseverance to find a solution.

When I was confronted with the definitive pronouncements that my physical difference precluded me from joining the military or the sheriff's department—paths I deeply desired to follow, inspired by my father's 49 years in the Army—these were not just minor hurdles. They were significant, seemingly insurmountable, obstacles. A fixed mindset might have sighed, shrugged, and accepted that verdict as a final, unchangeable limitation, a door permanently closed. The disappointment was crushing, believe me.

However, a growth mindset responds differently. It acknowledges the painful reality of the closed path but immediately begins to ask a new, empowering set of questions: "Okay, this particular avenue is not available. That stings. But what other paths can I explore, or more importantly, *create* for myself? How can I leverage my unique circumstances, the very things that seem like disadvantages, into unforeseen advantages or catalysts for innovation?"

Adopting this mindset doesn't magically insulate you from experiencing disappointment or frustration when things don't go as planned. That's part of the messy, beautiful human experience. But it *does* guarantee that you won't stay down for long. You persist with renewed determination, you adapt your strategies with newfound knowledge, and you learn continuously from every experience, effectively turning each challenge into a stepping stone rather than a stumbling block. This iterative process of

CHAPTER XII: How to Bounce Forward, Not Just Back

trying, learning, adapting, and trying again is the very engine of growth.

My groomsman, Bill Mitchell, a true testament to relentless determination, exemplifies this. Despite not being drafted into the NFL and facing constant "no's" from teams, he relentlessly pursued his dream of playing professional football, even resorting to cold-calling sports writers just to get direct contact with team personnel. Think about that level of grit! Bill describes challenges not as barriers, but as "information" that allows you to move forward, emphasizing that "success is the ability to go from failure to failure with enthusiasm." His incredible journey from a childhood in the South Bronx, balancing college with being a new father, to achieving his NFL dream, showcases an unwavering growth mindset. It's truly inspiring.

Setbacks as Setups for Greater Triumphs

My journey through life, marked by its unique contours and unexpected turns, has consistently, and often forcefully, reinforced a core philosophy for me: the **"Adapt and Overcome" model**. This isn't just a catchy phrase you put on a bumper sticker; it's a deeply lived reality that has taught me that setbacks, however painful or disruptive they may seem in the moment, are frequently disguised setups for greater, more meaningful achievements down the line.

That stinging "one-handed-monkey" taunt I endured on that second-grade kickball field was, by any measure, a deeply wounding setback. It possessed all the emotional ingredients to set me up for a life characterized by shame, social withdrawal, and a self-imposed ceiling on my potential. Instead, through a complex alchemy of searing pain, righteous indignation, and my mother's unwavering, almost fierce, belief in me, it became the unexpected setup for a fierce, lifelong determination to prove that perceived limitations are just that—perceptions, not immutable realities. Being born different, being thrust into a world that often demands conformity, and being relentlessly forced to "figure out a path for yourself," as I detailed extensively in the Introduction, wasn't ultimately a disadvantage. In fact, it was the very crucible, the intense forging ground, for developing profound adaptability, incredible resourcefulness, and a unique brand of innovation born from sheer necessity.

Consider again that significant financial investment—the $200,000 I poured into an array of prosthetic devices. Each device, each expenditure, was a tangible manifestation of a financial setback, a constant, gnawing reminder of what I perceived as a physical lack, a difference that needed "fixing" with external solutions. It was a dark, frustrating period.

However, this prolonged period of searching for external fixes, this costly journey of trying to bridge a perceived gap, ultimately led to a far more valuable and liberating profound realization: the empowering truth that "God already gave me everything that I need." This pivotal understanding wasn't just a comforting spiritual notion; it became the critical setup for a more authentic, resourceful, and internally driven way of living. It prompted a radical shift from relying on often cumbersome and expensive external crutches to discovering and trusting the inherent capabilities, the innate ingenuity, that resided within me all along. It was a revelation.

An old friend and "Life Can Change" guest, Angelo Lombardo, a highly successful Fortune 50 executive, describes a similar concept he calls "the gift of tragedy." When his infant daughter was born with a congenital heart defect, a life-threatening illness, it was, by any measure, a profound tragedy that brought him and his wife to their knees. He admitted to me, with immense vulnerability, that he often had to "fake it" and put on a brave face for his family and the medical staff, but he also allowed himself to "completely lose it" when alone, recognizing the importance of processing those crushing emotions. Yet, Angelo, with remarkable courage, found a gift within it: a profound shift in perspective. It forced him to re-evaluate his entire life, moving away from being a "Fortune 500 workaholic" driven by fear, and instead prioritizing what truly mattered—being present for his family. He realized that even in the midst of fire, there's a hidden gift waiting to be unwrapped, a lesson to propel you forward.

When you truly adopt and internalize an "Adapt and Overcome" philosophy, you begin to actively, almost instinctively, search for the hidden opportunity nestled within every apparent adversity. You train yourself to ask transformative questions: "How can this specific challenge, this unexpected obstacle, this painful experience, actually serve to make me stronger, wiser, more resourceful, or more compassionate? What invaluable lesson is disguised within this difficulty, and how can I use it to fuel my forward momentum?" This proactive reframing is the key to turning life's inevitable blows into powerful building blocks for your future success.

THE ISLAND
STRATEGIES

Actionable Strategies

Resilience isn't merely an innate, fixed trait that some are born with and others are not. No, it's a dynamic, multifaceted process and a robust set of skills that can be intentionally and systematically cultivated over time. It's about building an inner architecture that can not only withstand shocks but actually use their energy for growth.

Techniques for Emotional Regulation During Difficult Times:

Emotional storms are inevitable. We're human. The key isn't to suppress your emotions, to pretend they're not there, but to navigate them skillfully without being capsized.

- **Mindful Pausing (Creating the Gap):** When strong, overwhelming emotions like intense fear, surging anger, or profound despair arise, the practice of mindful pausing becomes your first line of defense. Instead of immediately reacting on autopilot, driven by the raw intensity of the feeling, intentionally create a small gap. Take a few slow, deep, deliberate breaths. Feel the air entering and leaving your body. Notice the physical sensations without judgment. This simple act of pausing creates a crucial space between the emotional trigger and your response, allowing you to access your higher-level thinking and choose how you wish to proceed, rather than being impulsively driven by the primal force of the emotion. This gap, my friend, is where your power of choice resides.

- **Name It to Tame It (The Power of Labeling):** Emotions can feel chaotic and utterly all-consuming when they are just a swirling mass of undifferentiated feeling. Acknowledging and gently labeling your emotions with specific words (e.g., "I am feeling overwhelmed and anxious right now," or "This is sadness I'm experiencing," or "There's a wave of frustration washing over me") can significantly reduce their intensity. This neurobiological trick, often referred to as "affect labeling," engages the prefrontal cortex, the more rational part of your brain, which helps to dampen the activity in the amygdala, the brain's emotional alarm center. It's like turning on a light in a dark, scary room; simply seeing what's there makes it less frightening and more manageable.

- **Perspective Shift (Zooming Out):** When you're in the thick of a difficult situation, it's incredibly easy to lose perspective; the problem can feel all-encompassing, like a giant shadow swallowing everything. Actively work to shift your perspective. Ask yourself clarifying questions: "In the grand scheme of my entire life, how much will this specific issue truly matter in five years? In one year? Even in one month?" Often, this contextualization shrinks the perceived size of the problem, making it feel less intimidating. Another powerful question is, "What is one small aspect of this situation that I can actually control or influence right now?" Focusing on your sphere of control, however small, powerfully counteracts feelings of helplessness.

- **Journaling (Externalizing and Processing):** The act of writing about your experiences, your swirling thoughts, and your feelings can be an incredibly effective tool for emotional regulation. It allows you to externalize what's stuck inside, giving it form and making it more tangible. As you write, you engage in a process of reflection and analysis that can lead to new insights, help you identify patterns in your emotional responses, and facilitate a much-needed emotional release. It's a safe, non-judgmental space to explore the nuances of your feelings and to begin to make sense of challenging experiences. It's a conversation with yourself, on paper.

Building Your Support System (Connection is Key, Even on Your Island):

The metaphor of the "Island of One" emphasizes self-responsibility, yes, but it does *not* advocate for isolation. Authentic, meaningful connection is a fundamental human need and a critical component of resilience. We are wired for connection.

- **Identify Your Anchors:** Consciously identify the people in your life who provide genuine support, understanding, and encouragement—these are your trusted friends, supportive family members, insightful mentors, or even like-minded groups and communities. These individuals are your anchors in stormy seas, the ones who help you stay grounded when everything else feels adrift.

- **Embrace Vulnerability (The Bridge to Connection):** Please, don't be afraid to be vulnerable with those you trust. Sharing your burdens, your fears, and your struggles doesn't make you weak; it makes you human and deeply relatable. It's often in these raw moments of shared vulnerability that the deepest connections are forged and the most meaningful support is truly received. Remember what I said earlier? Vulnerability is a strength, not a weakness.

My old buddy, Angelo, admitted to me that during his daughter's health crisis, he often had to "fake it" and put on a brave face for his family and the medical staff. But, crucially, he also allowed himself to "completely lose it" when alone, recognizing the importance of processing those crushing emotions. His willingness to share his deepest struggles, the raw truth of his fear and pain, created a profound connection with an audience member going through a similar heartbreaking situation, proving that shared vulnerability fosters profound understanding and empathy. It's an incredibly powerful bridge.

- **Reciprocity in Support (Giving and Receiving):** Resilience is also powerfully strengthened by *being* a source of support for others. When you offer a listening ear, heartfelt encouragement, or practical help to someone else navigating their own challenges, it not only benefits them but also reinforces your own sense of connection, purpose, and competence. Support is a beautiful, two-way street that enriches all involved.

The NFL Player's Wisdom: "You Must Have Short-Term Memory":

Bill Mitchell, that former NY Giants NFL player, a man I deeply respect and am proud to call one of my dearest and best friends who stood with me as a groomsman in my wedding, shared a profound piece of wisdom that extends far beyond the football field: "You must have Short Term Memory in order to make the next play." In the high-stakes, fast-paced world of professional sports, a quarterback can't afford to be mentally replaying an interception when he needs to lead a game-winning drive; a basketball player can't obsess over a missed free throw when the game is on the line again with seconds ticking down. That moment is gone. The next one is here.

This principle, my friend, is absolutely crucial for building deep resilience in life. Why? Because dwelling on mistakes, replaying setbacks endlessly, and allowing past missteps to dominate your mental landscape is like trying to sprint forward while dragging an increasingly heavy anchor. It relentlessly drains your vital energy, scatters your focus, and steals your capacity to engage fully and effectively with the present moment and the incredible opportunities it holds. The "what ifs" and "if onlys" become a paralyzing loop, a mental quicksand that sucks you deeper into past disappointments, preventing you from seeing clearly or acting decisively on the "next play" life inevitably presents.

This fixation on the past doesn't just cloud judgment; it erodes confidence and can even lead to a self-fulfilling prophecy where the fear of repeating a mistake actually *increases* the likelihood of doing so. This mental replaying reinforces neural pathways associated with the negative experience, making it emotionally "stickier" and harder to move past. The emotional residue of past errors can contaminate your perception of current opportunities, making you overly cautious, hesitant, or cynical, thus missing chances for success or joy. As the Japanese proverb states, "Fall seven times, stand up eight." It doesn't say "Fall seven times, and then replay all seven falls in agonizing detail forever."

- **Learn the Lesson with Precision, Then Let the Emotion Go:** This isn't a cursory glance at what went wrong; it's a focused, objective analysis of the setback, much like a team reviewing game footage. Ask rigorous questions: What were the precise contributing factors, both internal and external? What specific choices or actions, within my sphere of control, directly led to this undesirable outcome? What underlying assumptions, beliefs, or expectations did I hold that proved to be incorrect, incomplete, or unhelpful in this context? Were there external variables or unforeseen circumstances at play, and how might I better anticipate, prepare for, or mitigate such factors in the future? What alternative approaches could I have taken, and what might their likely outcomes have been?

Crucially, amidst all the data and reflection, what is the single most valuable piece of wisdom, the core actionable learning, the refined strategy, or the new perspective that I can extract from this experience that will serve me powerfully moving forward? It's vital to not just mentally acknowledge this lesson, but to write it down, to articulate it clearly, to discuss it with a trusted mentor if appropriate, and to consciously internalize it as a new piece of your operational toolkit. This is about the diligent work of extracting the critical signal—the actionable insight—from the often overwhelming surrounding noise of emotion, self-blame, and extraneous detail.

Once you've clearly identified these teachings and integrated them into your understanding and future strategies, the next, equally vital step is to consciously, deliberately work to release the emotional charge tied to the past event—the stinging regret that makes you second-guess yourself, the hot frustration that simmers beneath the surface, the cold grip of embarrassment that makes you want to hide, or the bitterness of anger that can poison your outlook. This isn't about suppressing legitimate feelings or pretending the pain didn't happen. It's about allowing yourself to feel those emotions fully, perhaps through journaling, talking with a confidant, physical activity, or creative expression—processing them through healthy outlets—and then making a conscious, empowered choice not to let those past emotions define your current state or hijack your future decisions.

This disciplined process differentiates true, constructive learning and growth from destructive rumination and wallowing. It's about transforming the raw, sometimes painful, data of a setback into refined, actionable intelligence for the future. This isn't about forgetting the event ever happened; a scar may remain as a reminder of the experience, a testament to what you've endured and learned, but it doesn't have to continuously ache or dictate your future movements and choices. It's about ensuring that the memory serves as a wise, albeit sometimes stern, advisor—offering valuable cautionary insights—not a relentless tormentor, a critical inner voice, or a crippling ghost from the past. The ultimate aim is to prevent past events, and their associated emotional baggage, from casting long, debilitating shadows that obscure your path forward and keep you from making that courageous, clear-headed next play with the clarity, confidence, and full presence it demands and deserves.

By redefining failure, cultivating a growth mindset, embracing the "adapt and overcome" philosophy, and actively employing these strategies, you build an increasingly powerful Resilience Engine. You learn not just to bounce back, but to bounce *forward*, transforming every challenge into a stepping stone on your path to thriving. This is not merely survival; it is evolution. And it's an evolution you are more than capable of.

CHAPTER XIII

You are Built to Thrive

"You are already built to thrive. This isn't a state you need to achieve through endless striving or external acquisition. It is a present reality, woven into the very fabric of your being, waiting to be fully uncovered and owned."

Fully Owning Your Magnificent Design!

Throughout this incredible journey we've shared, we've explored the keys to unlocking your potential, navigating the unique landscape of your "Island of One," and diligently building your resilience. Now, we arrive at what I believe is the most profound and liberating truth of all: You are *already* built to thrive. This isn't some distant state you need to achieve through endless striving, through constantly pushing harder, or through acquiring more external things. No, my friend. It is a present reality, woven into the very fabric of your being, waiting—patiently—to be fully uncovered, embraced, and owned by you.

Internalizing the Core Message:
"God Already Gave What You Need"

This statement has been a recurring theme, a consistent drumbeat through these pages, and for good reason. It is, quite simply, the cornerstone of understanding your inherent capacity. "God already gave what you need to do what He wants you to do." Your unique gifts, that incredible capacity for choice you wield, your innate resilience—these are not additions you must desperately seek out, like rare artifacts. No, they are powerful endowments you already possess. They are your original equipment, installed at birth.

Internalizing this message means making a radical shift in your mindset: moving from a place of perceived lack to one of profound abundance. It means truly recognizing that the essential tools for a purposeful and meaningful life were part of your original package.

My journey of spending over my hard earned cash on prosthetics, only to realize I could fly, play golf, and live fully using the capabilities I was born with, was a profound, deeply humbling, and ultimately liberating lesson in this. For so long, those "devices" were an attempt to compensate for a perceived deficit, a flaw in my design. The truth was, the essential "device"—my inherent adaptability, my stubborn determination, my relentless spirit—was already within me. The revelation was almost overwhelming. Your perceived limitations, those things you might lament or wish away, are often the very circumstances that will force you to uncover these deep, inherent strengths. It turns out, you were packed with everything you needed for the adventure, even if you thought you needed a bigger, fancier suitcase. You just had to look inside yourself.

Let's think of some more examples of this "God Already Gave What You Need" truth in action:

- **Your Personal Example:** Recall that incredibly powerful moment, after extensive investment in prosthetics, when you truly discovered you could fly an airplane and play golf with the capabilities you were born with. This was a profound, almost spiritual, realization that the "devices" you sought externally were not essential. Instead, your inherent adaptability, your determination, and your spirit were the true tools. This illustrates how "God already gave what you need" by equipping you with an incredible inner resilience and resourcefulness that no external aid could truly replicate. It was a beautiful, hard-won epiphany.

- **The Unemployed Artist:** Imagine Sarah, a truly talented painter, struggling for years to find gallery representation. The rejection was soul-crushing, and she felt like a failure. Instead of giving up, she had a moment of profound clarity: she already possessed the creativity, the fierce determination, and the communication skills to connect with her audience directly. She didn't need a gatekeeper. She started an online store, marketed her work beautifully on social media, and slowly but surely, built a thriving community around her art. She proved that the "gallery" she thought she needed was already within her capacity to create and connect.

- **The Aspiring Entrepreneur:** Think of Alex, who dreamed of starting a business but felt utterly limited by a lack of capital and connections. He saw only obstacles. Instead of waiting indefinitely for an external investor, he tapped into his innate problem-solving abilities, his natural resourcefulness, and a strong, ingrained work ethic. He started tiny, leveraged his existing skills, and gradually, patiently, built his business from the ground up. He proved that the greatest "investment" was his own inherent drive and ingenuity, already there, waiting to be unleashed.

This truth is powerfully demonstrated by my guest on "Life Can Change," Josh Roche. He went from literally living homeless in a Honda Civic as a teenager, with no formal marketing education whatsoever, to becoming a Chief Marketing Officer for a major organization and building his own successful consulting organization and e-commerce companies. Josh didn't wait for external qualifications or capital; he "accepted and learned how to do it after," driven by an innate, almost desperate, desire for freedom and a relentless focus on getting "better results" than anyone else. His story underscores that the essential "tools" for success were always within him, dormant perhaps, but always present.

Celebrating Your Uniqueness: Your Island as a Testament to Your Design

Your "Island of One," with all its unique challenges, its specific terrain, and its sometimes rocky characteristics, is not a place of deficit. It is not a mistake in the grand, intricate design of your life. Quite the opposite. It is a testament to your unique blueprint for success and contribution. The very things that make you different, the experiences that have shaped your specific landscape, are precisely what equip you with a distinctive perspective and a truly unique set of strengths.

As I shared in the Introduction, "My experience with one hand... became the unconventional lens through which I stumbled upon a fundamental and profoundly liberating truth: we are all, in fact, 'born with everything you need to live a life of purpose and meaning.'" My "island," with all its apparent limitations, didn't hinder me. It *forced* innovation. It *demanded* creativity. It cultivated a depth of empathy born from intimately understanding struggle.

So, I ask you: what is *your* island teaching you? How have your unique circumstances, those things that set you apart, forged strengths that others may not possess to the same degree? Celebrating your uniqueness means seeing your island not as a barrier, not as a flaw, but as your personal training ground, perfectly designed to sculpt the magnificent individual you are truly meant to be.

Let's explore some more examples of how your "island" is actually a testament to your magnificent design:

- **Your Personal Example:** Your "island" of experience with one hand has uniquely equipped you. It has not only forced innovation and creativity in navigating daily life but has also forged a profound depth of empathy born from understanding struggle. This unique perspective allows you to connect with others on a deeper level and share a message of inherent capability that resonates far beyond conventional wisdom. It's not a limitation; it's your superpower of understanding.

- **The Introverted Leader:** Maria always felt her introversion was a hindrance to leadership. She saw it as a weakness in a world that often celebrated extroversion. However, her "island" of quiet reflection allowed her to develop exceptional listening skills, a deep, intuitive understanding of her team's individual needs, and the quiet ability to make incredibly well-thought-out decisions. She discovered that her unique approach fostered a more empathetic and effective leadership style than her more outwardly boisterous colleagues. Her introversion wasn't a flaw; it was the source of her distinct leadership gift.

- **The Rural Upbringing:** John, who grew up on a farm, initially felt completely out of place in the fast-paced, cutthroat city. He felt unsophisticated. Yet, his "island" had instilled in him an unparalleled work ethic, incredibly practical problem-solving skills, and a deep appreciation for the cycles of growth and resilience—qualities often lacking in his urban counterparts. These seemingly "simple" qualities made him an invaluable asset in his urban startup, where others often lacked his grounded perspective and tenacity. His rural roots were his secret strength.

- **The Chronic Illness Survivor:** Lisa's battle with a chronic illness was her "island." While it presented immense physical challenges and daily pain, it also cultivated in her an extraordinary level of patience, profound self-awareness, and an unwavering commitment to advocating for herself and others. She became a powerful voice for patient empowerment, transforming her personal struggle into a platform for positive change and deep empathy. Her illness, though arduous, became the forge for her advocacy.

The Shift from External Validation to Internal Knowing

So much of our lives, if we're honest, can be spent chasing external validation—the elusive approval from others, shiny societal accolades, the fleeting material symbols of success. We constantly look *outside* ourselves for confirmation of our worth, for proof that we're "good enough." But the journey to truly, fully owning your magnificent design involves a fundamental, deeply liberating shift: moving from frantically seeking external validation to patiently cultivating an **internal knowing**.

This "internal knowing" isn't some abstract concept; it's the deep, unshakeable conviction of your own inherent worth and strength, completely independent of outside approval or fluctuating circumstances. It's understanding, deep in your bones, that your value is not contingent on your achievements, your appearance, or what anyone else thinks of you. It is intrinsic. It simply *is*. When you truly operate from this powerful place of internal knowing, you are no longer buffeted by the often-fickle opinions of others or the unpredictable ups and downs of external events. Your anchor, finally, is within.

This doesn't mean you become immune to feedback or indifferent to connection. Not at all. It means your fundamental sense of self is not *dependent* on these external factors. You can engage with the world from a place of solidity, knowing your core worth is intact, regardless of what's happening around you. It's like having an unshakeable foundation for your "Island of One."

Let's look at more examples of this powerful shift to internal knowing:

- **Your Personal Example:** In your public speaking or advocacy, the shift from seeking approval for "overcoming a challenge" to speaking from a place of deep, inherent truth about human potential exemplifies internal knowing. When you share your story, the true power comes not from the audience's reaction to your "disability," but from your unshakeable conviction in the message of inherent capability. It's a strength you now possess independent of external validation, and that's why it resonates so deeply.

- **The Performer's True Joy:** Imagine a musician who once sought validation solely from roaring applause and record sales. After experiencing deep burnout and a profound sense of emptiness, she shifted her focus. She reconnected with the intrinsic, pure joy of creating music, finding fulfillment in the process itself, regardless of external reception. Her performances became more authentic, more soulful, and far more powerful because they flowed from an internal wellspring of passion, not from a desperate need for applause.

- **The CEO's Quiet Confidence:** A highly successful CEO initially felt the constant pressure to prove himself to demanding shareholders and relentless competitors. He was constantly striving. Through deep self-reflection and a deepening understanding of his true values, he realized his worth wasn't in the numbers. His true worth lay in his integrity, his ability to inspire his team, and his unwavering commitment to ethical leadership. This internal knowing allowed him to navigate difficult business decisions with calm conviction, completely unswayed by public opinion or fleeting market trends.

- **The Athlete's Inner Drive:** A professional athlete, after a career-ending injury, found her identity had been too closely tied to her athletic achievements. The loss of her sport felt like the loss of herself. By cultivating internal knowing, she discovered that her strength, her discipline, and her competitive spirit were not limited to the playing field but were inherent, transferable qualities that could be applied to new endeavors. This allowed her to thrive in entirely new ways, finding fulfillment beyond the roar of the crowd.

This is beautifully illustrated by Bill Mitchell, my dear friend and former NFL player. His journey to the New York Giants was fueled by a deep, internal desire to be great for his young daughter, not just for external accolades. Similarly, my good friend Chip Yates, told by a psychologist in his youth that he wouldn't amount to anything, found an internal fire lit by that negative pronouncement, which propelled him to achieve 18 world records. It's a powerful reminder that true motivation often comes from within, despite what anyone else might say or believe.

THE ISLAND
STRATEGIES

Actionable Strategies: Owning Your Design

So, how do we actively, consistently, cultivate this profound internal knowing and fully own our magnificent design? It's a daily practice, a gentle yet persistent turning inward.

Practices for Cultivating Self-Compassion and Self-Acceptance:

Emotional storms are inevitable. We're human. The key isn't to suppress your emotions, to pretend they're not there, but to navigate them skillfully without being capsized.

- **Treat Yourself as You Would a Good Friend:** This is simple, but revolutionary. When you make a mistake, or when that ugly voice of self-doubt starts whispering about how inadequate you are, *pause*. Then, offer yourself the same kindness, understanding, and encouragement you would offer a cherished friend in a similar situation.
    - **Example:** Instead of thinking, "I'm so stupid for missing that deadline, I always mess things up," try, "It's okay. Everyone makes mistakes sometimes, and this is a learning opportunity. What can I learn from this, and how can I support myself to do better next time without burning out?"

- **Mindful Self-Awareness:** Just notice. Acknowledge your perceived flaws and imperfections without harsh judgment. Recognize that these are simply part of the messy, beautiful human experience. We all have them.
    - **Example:** If you notice a sudden wave of insecurity about your appearance before a big event, simply observe it without adding judgment like "I shouldn't feel this way, it's silly." Just acknowledge, "Ah, I'm feeling insecure about my appearance right now. That's interesting." The act of observing without judgment lessens its power.

- **Challenge Your Inner Critic:** Become acutely aware of that negative, often harsh, voice within. It's loud, isn't it? Question its pronouncements. Is it truly speaking the truth, or is it just echoing old, unhelpful scripts you picked up along the way? (This is where Key #7, Reshaping Your Beliefs, comes in handy).
    - **Example:** When your inner critic screeches, "You're not good enough to try that, you'll fail just like last time," pause. Then ask yourself: "Is that *truly* a fact, or is it just a fear-based thought, an old echo? What evidence do I have to the contrary? What *can* I do?"

- **Practice Gratitude for Yourself:** Take time, intentionally, to acknowledge your efforts, your inherent strengths, and the progress you've already made, no matter how small it seems.
    - **Example:** At the end of each day, mentally (or even better, physically) list three things you appreciate about yourself, not just what you *did*, but who you *are*. Such as, "I'm grateful for my persistence in tackling that difficult task today," or "I'm thankful for my ability to listen patiently and truly hear my friend today," or "I appreciate my courage for trying something new."

Journaling Prompts to Acknowledge and Celebrate Your Progress and Strengths:

These prompts are designed to get you thinking, to help you uncover and articulate the incredible person you already are. Grab a pen and just write, without judgment.

- "What is one challenge I have overcome that demonstrates my resilience, even when I felt like giving up?"
    - **Example Response:** "Overcoming the intense fear of public speaking in my last presentation really showed me how resilient I am. My heart was pounding, but I pushed through, and it felt amazing to connect with my audience from a place of authenticity, despite my nerves."

- "What unique perspective or skill do I possess *because* of my specific life experiences (my 'island')? How has it shaped me?"
    - **Example Response:** "Growing up in a multicultural household, navigating two very different ways of seeing the world, gave me a unique ability to bridge communication gaps and understand diverse viewpoints. It's invaluable in my team-oriented work; I can see all sides."

- "Write a letter to my younger self, acknowledging their inherent worth and the strengths they possess that will see them through any challenge."
    - **Example Content:** "Dear Younger Self, I know you feel awkward and unsure right now, always feeling like you don't quite fit in. But please know that your quiet nature is actually a superpower of observation. Your sensitivity will become your greatest empathy, allowing you to connect deeply with others. Your endless curiosity will lead you to incredible discoveries. You are already enough, exactly as you are, and you are far stronger than

you know."

- "What am I most proud of about myself, not for an achievement or something I *did*, but for who I am as a person?"
    - **Example Response:** "I'm most proud of my unwavering commitment to integrity, even when it's difficult and uncomfortable. And I'm proud of my capacity for genuine compassion towards others, especially when they're struggling."

- "How can I reframe a perceived 'weakness' or 'difference' into a unique strength or asset *today*?"
    - **Example Response:** "My perceived 'stubbornness' that others sometimes comment on? I can reframe that as unwavering determination when pursuing a goal I truly believe in. Today, I'll apply that determination to finally finishing that personal project I've been procrastinating on, and not stop until it's done."

Creating a "Thrive Manifesto" for Your Life:

A "Thrive Manifesto" is your deeply personal declaration of your core truths, your unwavering values, and your fierce commitments to living a life aligned with your magnificent design. It's your inner constitution.

Content Ideas:

- **Statements affirming your inherent worth:** (e.g., "I am inherently worthy and deserving of love, joy, and abundance. My very existence is a precious gift, and I embrace it fully.")

- **Declarations of your core gifts and strengths:** (e.g., "My unique creativity is a powerful force for good, bringing beauty and innovation into the world, shaping ideas into reality. My profound capacity for compassion allows me to connect deeply and authentically with others, offering comfort and understanding.")

- **Commitments to self-care and self-compassion:** (e.g., "I commit to treating myself with unwavering kindness and understanding, nurturing my mind, body, and spirit with gentle care. I will honor my needs and boundaries, knowing that they are essential for my well-being.")

- **Your personal definition of thriving:** (e.g., "For me, thriving means living each day with purpose, courage, and authentic connection, using my unique talents and experiences to serve others and to experience profound, soul-deep joy.")

- **A reminder of your power to choose:** (e.g., "I am the courageous captain of my choices and the deliberate architect of my reality, empowered to respond to life's inevitable challenges with wisdom, grace, and unwavering resolve.")

Example of a "Thrive Manifesto" snippet:

"I am a beacon of light, uniquely designed for a life of profound impact. My greatest strength lies in my willingness to be vulnerable, my deepest wisdom is found in my experiences, and my true purpose blossoms from my

authentic self. I am inherently worthy of love, abundance, and joy, not because of what I achieve, but simply because of who I inherently am. I choose courage over comfort, growth over stagnation, and love over fear, every single day. I will nurture my spirit, honor my body, and engage my mind, knowing that every aspect of my being is a testament to my magnificent design. I am built to thrive, and I choose to live that truth, fully and unapologetically, every single day."

Write it down, decorate it, make it beautiful, and place it somewhere you can see it daily. Let it be a living document that constantly inspires and guides you. Consider reading it aloud each morning as a powerful, personal affirmation. Let the words sink into your bones.

You, my friend, are not a broken project waiting to be fixed. You are a magnificent design waiting to be discovered, embraced, and fully lived. The journey we've been on together, and the one that continues, is about peeling away the layers of doubt, the societal conditioning, and the limiting beliefs to reveal the brilliance that has been there all along. When you fully own this truth, when it sinks into your deepest core, you truly become unstoppable. As the incomparable Oprah Winfrey reminds us, "The greatest discovery of all time is that a person can change his future by merely changing his attitude." And that attitude begins with knowing you are already built to thrive.

PART IV

Beyond Your Island - Connecting, Contributing, and Continuing The Journey

Island of One: Born Different. Build to Thrive

CHAPTER XIV
Your Island as a Beacon

"To help people live their lives deliberately, discover their true purpose and act as a beacon of encouragement for lasting change.."

Shining Your Light for Others

The journey we've taken together—embracing your "Island of One," fully owning your unique design, and recognizing your inherent capacity to thrive—is, without question, a deeply personal and introspective odyssey. It has demanded courage, quiet self-reflection, and a willingness to confront your innermost fears and those stubborn limiting beliefs. It can feel like a solitary path, can't it?

Yet, here's one of the most beautiful and profound paradoxes of this inward journey: it doesn't lead to greater isolation. Quite the opposite. This profound self-acceptance and newfound inner strength are precisely what equip you most powerfully to forge authentic, meaningful connections with others and to make a lasting, positive impact on the world around you.

Your island, which once might have felt like a solitary outpost, a symbol of your separateness or struggle, can be transformed. It can become a radiant beacon, its steady light cutting through the fog, guiding and inspiring others who are still endeavoring to navigate their own turbulent waters and discover the shores of their own inherent potential. This chapter is all about how your personal thriving becomes a powerful catalyst for connection and contribution. As the poet John Donne famously wrote, "No man is an island entire of itself; every man is a piece of the continent, a part of the main." We are all connected, and your light can illuminate the way for others.

Authentic Connection from a Place of Wholeness, Not Lack

There's a pervasive and often unexamined misconception in our culture that true strength equates to complete self-sufficiency, a kind of rugged individualism that borders on emotional aloofness. We're sometimes taught that needing others is a weakness, that asking for help is a sign of failure. But the authentic strength forged in the fires of your unique "Island of One" journey—the resilience, self-awareness, and acceptance you've cultivated—fosters not a withdrawal from connection, but a significantly deeper and more authentic capacity for it.

When you no longer desperately seek external validation to fill some internal void, when your sense of self-worth is deeply anchored within, you approach relationships from a place of profound wholeness, not from a place of aching neediness or scarcity. This changes *everything*.

- **Authenticity Breeds Connection: The Courage to Be Real**
When you truly own your story—your triumphs, yes, but also your struggles, your imperfections, your vulnerabilities—you become exponentially more real, more human, and therefore, more relatable to others. Vulnerability, which is so often feared as a sign of weakness or an open invitation for judgment, actually becomes the most powerful bridge to genuine human connection. As I've often shared, and believe with every fiber of my being, "Vulnerability is the key to success." And it is, without a doubt, the absolute key to authentic connection.

When you have the courage to drop the carefully constructed facade, the mask you might wear to appear "perfect" or "unscathed," you create a safe space that implicitly invites others to do the same. This mutual unveiling of true selves is where real intimacy and understanding can finally blossom. Think of the profound relief and connection you feel when someone else dares to share a struggle you've also faced silently; your act of authentic sharing can offer that same priceless gift to others.

For example, sharing your past financial anxieties, rather than meticulously projecting an image of constant financial success, can open up honest conversations and create deep, empathetic bonds with others who are navigating similar concerns. It's often in our shared imperfections that we find our greatest connection. I've even shared a deeply personal, even embarrassing, story about wetting my pants as a child while playing Atari, too engrossed in the game to stop. I share this in front of thousands of people, not because I enjoy the embarrassment, but because it's a part of my core, and it shows the power of being vulnerable to connect with others on a profoundly human level.

- **From Scarcity to Abundance in Relationships: Giving from a Full Cup** If your fundamental needs for esteem, self-acceptance, and love are met primarily from within, your entire orientation towards relationships shifts dramatically. You no longer enter into connections— whether friendships, romantic partnerships, or professional collaborations—with an unconscious (or conscious) agenda of finding someone to "complete" you, to "fix" your perceived brokenness, or to validate your very existence. This scarcity mindset in relationships often manifests as clinginess, jealousy, possessiveness, or a constant, nagging fear of abandonment, because your sense of self is precariously tied to the other person's approval or presence. It's exhausting, for everyone involved.

  However, when you operate from a place of inner wholeness, you approach relationships with an abundance mentality. You have a full cup, and you seek to share your journey, your joys, and your strengths, while also being genuinely open to receiving the unique gifts and support of others. Relationships become about co-creation, mutual growth, and shared experiences, rather than a desperate attempt to fill a personal deficit. You connect because you *want* to, because it brings you joy, not because you *need* to in order to feel okay about yourself. It's a completely different dynamic.

- **Clearer Boundaries, Deeper Bonds: The Strength of Self-Respect** Understanding your own needs, your core values, and your inherent worth is the bedrock upon which you can build and maintain healthy boundaries. These boundaries aren't walls designed to keep people out; they are more like well-defined property lines that communicate self-respect and clearly delineate what is acceptable and unacceptable in your interactions. This clarity, far from pushing people away, actually fosters a deeper level of respect and allows for more honest, secure, and ultimately, more intimate engagement.

    When people know where you stand, when they understand that you value yourself enough to have clear lines, they are far more likely to treat you with the consideration you deserve. Unclear or non-existent boundaries often lead to resentment, misunderstanding, and a messy "enmeshment" that erodes the very foundation of any relationship. Healthy boundaries, paradoxically, create the safety and trust necessary for true closeness and deeper bonds to form. For instance, clearly communicating your need for personal quiet time without guilt, rather than silently resenting intrusions, allows for relationships where both individuals' needs are respected and honored.

Embracing your "Island of One" and the deep, internal work it entails means you are no longer adrift in the vast ocean of life, desperately seeking rescue or validation from external sources. You become a sovereign territory, secure in your own worth and capabilities, and from this empowered stance, you are capable of forming healthy, interdependent alliances based on mutual respect, shared values, and a genuine desire for authentic connection. It's a beautiful thing to witness, and to experience.

How Your Story Can Inspire and Support Others on Their Own Islands

Your journey of resilience, the specific narrative of how you've navigated the unique terrain of your personal "Island of One," is far more than just your individual history. It is a powerful, living testament to the strength and adaptability of the human spirit. The challenges you have faced, the obstacles you have overcome, often with great effort and ingenuity, and the hard-won wisdom you have painstakingly gained along the way—these are not treasures to be hoarded solely for your own benefit. Oh no. They hold immense potential to inspire, to encourage, to offer practical guidance, and to instill profound hope in others who are currently grappling with their own islands, perhaps feeling lost, overwhelmed, or profoundly alone in their experiences.

- **Shared Humanity in Struggle: Finding Universality in the Particular** When you choose to courageously share your vulnerabilities—the raw moments of doubt, the times you stumbled, the fears you confronted—alongside your victories, you tap into a deep well of shared human experience. Others see their own struggles, their own private battles, reflected in your story. They realize, perhaps for the very first time, that they are not alone in their anxieties, their perceived limitations, or their feelings of inadequacy. This recognition can be incredibly empowering, breaking the chains of isolation that often accompany personal challenges.

My story of being born with one hand is, in its specifics,

unique to me. But the underlying themes—of overcoming adversity, of challenging and redefining limitations, of making conscious choices in response to incredibly difficult circumstances—these are universal narratives that resonate across a wide spectrum of human experience. Someone struggling with a chronic illness, a devastating career setback, a difficult family situation, or a crisis of faith can find powerful echoes of their own journey in the principles of resilience and adaptation I share. Your specific island may be unique, but the human experience of navigating challenges on it is universal.

- **The Power of Embodiment** Your life, as you actively apply the principles of thriving, becomes a tangible, breathing demonstration of what is truly possible. When others witness you navigating your challenges with courage, adapting to setbacks with grace, and continuing to grow despite obstacles, it ignites a spark of hope within them. It provides concrete, undeniable evidence that they, too, possess the capacity to navigate their own difficulties and to uncover their own dormant strengths. You become a living embodiment of the principles you've embraced, far more persuasive than any abstract theory or secondhand account. Your actions, your attitude, and your very presence can communicate a powerful message: "If I can do this, with my unique set of challenges, then you, with yours, can find your way too." This isn't about presenting a false image of perfection; it's an honest portrayal of consistent progress through fierce persistence.

- **Sharing Field-Tested Tools** The strategies you have developed and employed to reframe failure, to build and sustain your resilience engine, to master your time

CHAPTER XIV: Your Island as a Beacon

effectively, or to reshape your limiting beliefs are not just abstract theories culled from books; they are field-tested tools, honed and validated in the demanding laboratory of your own life. Sharing these practical insights—the specific techniques that truly worked for you, the mental shifts that made a profound difference, the resources you found helpful—can provide an invaluable lifeline to someone else who is desperately searching for answers or a way forward. This could be as simple as sharing a coping mechanism for anxiety that you found effective, explaining precisely how you broke down an overwhelming goal into manageable steps, or offering your perspective on how to reframe a common limiting belief. Your lived experience gives your advice an authenticity and credibility that can be profoundly impactful.

This brings me to the incredible individuals I had the profound privilege of interviewing and learning from on my self-produced television talk show, "Life Can Change." For a dozen impactful episodes, which premiered on Amazon Prime, I aimed to bring authentic stories of transformation to a wide audience. At one point, I even had the opportunity to take the show to a major network, but I ultimately made the conscious, difficult decision to step away. I felt that I wasn't in a place in my life to truly give the maximum impact to people through my experiences, and honestly, I really wanted to do something great for my family, which eventually led me to start my wine business, McClain Cellars. While the show's run was shorter than it could have been, it was truly amazing and incredibly impactful, and through it, I met a lot of remarkable people. You can even find details about the show and my unfinished book, also titled "Life Can Change: Turning Obstacles into Opportunities," online if you're curious.

Despite the pivot in my career path, the wisdom shared by these guests remains a cornerstone of my own journey and the insights I share with you today. They are truly exemplary figures who embody the principles of thriving through adversity, and their stories are worth hearing:

- **Chip Yates:** A pioneering inventor and my good friend, Chip holds an astounding 18 Guinness World Records, including for the fastest electric airplane and motorcycle. Imagine being told by a psychologist in your youth that you wouldn't amount to anything, as Chip was. Yet, he pushed through, breaking bones in motorcycle accidents and facing terrifying moments where batteries blew up in his experimental aircraft. Chip's story screams of the profound "audacity to try, the courage to fail, and the willingness to learn from every setback." He candidly shared how even getting fired from a job he hated was, in hindsight, "a huge favor" that compelled him to reclaim his time and pursue his passions, ultimately leading to unparalleled achievements. His willingness to embrace discomfort and failure is a masterclass in resilience.

- **Bill Mitchell:** A former NFL player for the New York Giants and one of my dearest friends, who stood with me as a groomsman in my wedding, Bill's journey is a powerful testament to relentless tenacity. He grew up in the South Bronx with a single mother, became a new father at 17 while in college, and famously walked onto an NFL team despite countless rejections and people telling him it was impossible. His core belief that challenges are simply "information" to be acted upon, and that "success is the ability to go from failure to failure with enthusiasm," is a guiding principle that propelled him to professional

CHAPTER XIV: Your Island as a Beacon

football and beyond. His dedication to surrounding himself with "healthy people" and his consistent practice of "getting up before the birds" every single day reveal a character built on incredible discipline and unwavering optimism. He's a true force of nature.

- **Josh Roche:** My guest on "Life Can Change," Josh's incredible transformation is a true rags-to-riches story that still gives me chills. He went from literally living homeless in a Honda Civic as a teenager, with literally no formal marketing education, to becoming a Chief Marketing Officer for a major organization and a successful entrepreneur with his own consulting business and e-commerce companies. Josh illustrates the profound power of intentional action, developing consistent routines (like daily meditation, even when life was chaotic), and striving for "better results" rather than just "working harder." His core drive for freedom, and his ability to be proactive rather than reactive, are hallmarks of his remarkable character and a powerful lesson for us all.

- **Angelo Lombardo:** A highly respected Fortune 50 executive and a courageous man I've had the honor of calling a friend, Angelo's story is one of profound resilience in the face of deep family tragedy. When his infant daughter was born with a life-threatening congenital heart defect, a crisis that truly brought him and his wife to their knees with fear and grief, he discovered what he calls "the gift of tragedy"—a perspective that forced him to re-evaluate his entire life. He stepped away from being a "Fortune 500 workaholic" driven by fear, and instead prioritized what truly mattered—being present for his family. His candid admission of having to "fake it" to maintain composure for others, and his belief that "real change comes from tiny, consistent actions" offer deep, relatable wisdom for anyone facing life's most challenging moments.

Your island, therefore, doesn't have to remain a solitary, isolated entity. By courageously and generously shining the light of your experience, your struggles, and your triumphs, you help to illuminate the often-confusing and challenging paths for others. You become a guide, a source of encouragement, and a powerful reminder of the resilient strength that lies within every human heart. As Robert Ingersoll eloquently put it, "We rise by lifting others." And by lifting others, you inevitably lift yourself even higher.

The Deep Fulfillment That Comes from Using Your Unique Gifts and Experiences to Make a Positive Impact

One of the most profound and enduring human needs, as identified by thinkers from Abraham Maslow to modern positive psychologists, is the need for contribution—that innate desire to make a positive impact, to add real value to the lives of others, to leave a legacy, however small or grand. As you increasingly embrace your own thrive-ability and step into your inherent power, you will likely find that a natural and compelling urge arises: to use your unique gifts, your hard-won experiences, and your authentic self to serve something larger than yourself. This, my friend, is where deep, truly sustainable purpose and fulfillment are often found. It's the ultimate expression of your magnificent design.

- **Your Unique Gifts are Meant to be Shared** The treasures you have meticulously unearthed on your island such as your specific talents, your cultivated resilience, your heightened creativity born from constraint, your profound empathy shaped by your own understanding of struggle, your unique perspectives forged by your individual journey—these are not meant to be kept solely for your own benefit or enjoyment. Oh no. They are valuable resources that possess the power to enrich the lives of others, to solve problems, to inspire change, and to alleviate suffering. Recognizing that your gifts have a purpose beyond your personal advancement can be a powerful motivator for contribution.

For example, if your journey has gifted you with exceptional problem-solving skills, you might find profound purpose in mentoring young entrepreneurs, guiding them through the pitfalls you've already navigated. If your struggles have cultivated deep empathy, you might be powerfully drawn to volunteer work that supports those in vulnerable situations, understanding their pain on a visceral level. My own deep passion for writing, which I engaged in as a child, and my unwavering love for teaching are direct expressions of my gifts, and I find immense, soul-satisfying fulfillment in sharing them to impact others. It's where my energy truly comes alive.

- **The Joyful Expression of Your Authentic Self** True, sustainable fulfillment in contribution rarely comes from a sense of grim obligation or dutiful martyrdom. It blossoms most vibrantly when your efforts to contribute are deeply aligned with what genuinely makes you "sing, dream, and cry"—those core passions and values we identified earlier. When your acts of service are an authentic expression of who you are and what you care about most deeply, they cease to feel like work. They become, instead, a joyful and energizing extension of your being. This alignment ensures that your contributions are not only impactful but also personally nourishing, preventing burnout and fostering a powerful sense of intrinsic reward.

If your passion is teaching, your contribution might be through formal education or informal mentoring, sharing what you know. If you love nature, your contribution could involve environmental advocacy or conservation efforts, protecting what you cherish. The key is to find the overlap between your gifts, your passions, and the needs of the world.

- **The Exponential Power of Positive Impact** It is crucial to remember that the positive impact you make, even if it seems small or localized to one person or one situation, can create ripples that extend far beyond your immediate perception. Like a pebble dropped into a still pond, your act of kindness, your shared wisdom, your empowering encouragement can set in motion a chain of positive consequences that you may never fully witness.

Helping one individual find their strength, discover their purpose, or overcome a significant obstacle can empower *them* to, in turn, positively influence their own families, their communities, and their workplaces. This exponential nature of positive impact is one of the most beautiful aspects of contribution. Never, ever underestimate the power of a single life—your life—to touch and transform many others. Your light, once shining for you, can become a guiding star for so many more.

CHAPTER XIV: Your Island as a Beacon

A Guiding Example of Purpose in Action

To illustrate how these powerful concepts of connection and contribution can crystallize into a guiding framework for your life, I'll share my own personal mission statement once more. This statement, which I often refer to in my seminars, truly serves as my unwavering North Star:

"To help people live their lives deliberately, discover their true purpose and act as a beacon of encouragement for lasting change."

This mission statement is far more than just a collection of well-intentioned words; it is a direct and deeply personal distillation of my own journey on my "Island of One," and it informs how I strive to engage with the world every single day:

- **"Live their lives deliberately"**: This component directly reflects my profound understanding of the immense power of choice, the absolute necessity of intentional living (as explored in Key #4: Charting Your Course), and the transformative potential of conscious action (Key #10: The Alchemy of Action). It's about empowering others to move from being passive recipients of life's circumstances to becoming active architects of their desired reality. It's about waking people up to their own power.

- **"Discover their true purpose"**: This resonates deeply with the journey of unearthing innate gifts (Key #1) and encouraging individuals to align their lives with what truly makes them come alive, what gives their existence meaning and passion, what makes their heart sing. It's about guiding others to listen to that quiet inner voice, that unique calling that resides within their own "Island of

One."

- **"Act as a beacon of encouragement for lasting change"**: This is the very essence of transforming personal struggle into shared strength. It's about using my own messy, beautiful story, the lessons learned from navigating my physical difference and other life challenges, and the insights gained from applying the 7 Keys, to inspire, guide, and support others as they work to reshape their own beliefs (Key #7) and build their own resilience engines (Chapter 11). It's about being a consistent source of light and hope, demonstrating that change is not only possible but an inherent human capacity, woven into our very being.

This mission statement is far more than just a collection of well-intentioned words; it is the operational compass that guides my decisions, shapes my work, and defines how I endeavor to show up in the world authentically and with impact. It's the conscious articulation of how I aim to make my own island, with its unique history and perspectives, a beacon of hope and empowerment for others.

So, I ask you now: what is the unique mission that is calling to you from the very heart of your island? How can your distinct journey, your resilience forged in your specific fires, and your hard-won wisdom serve as a guiding light for others who may be navigating similar paths or facing their own daunting challenges? The deepest and most enduring fulfillment often lies not merely in achieving our own thriving, but in extending our hand and bravely sharing our light to help others thrive too. This, my friend, is the ultimate expression of our interconnectedness, and it's a profound joy.

CHAPTER XV: Living a Life of Purpose and Meaning, Every Single Day

CHAPTER XV
Living a Life of Purpose and Meaning, Every Single Day

"Remove the word 'Later' from your vocabulary as it is the worst killer of a dream"

The Unstoppable You

You've made it. You have journeyed through the very core of your being, traversing the beautiful, sometimes challenging, landscapes of your **Gifts**, the profound preciousness of your **Time**, the rich lessons of your **Past**, the clear direction of your **Plan**, the honest truth of your **Needs**, the often-whispering nature of your **Fears**, and the very architecture of your **Beliefs**. You have begun the profound and truly transformative work of building unwavering resilience and fully owning the magnificent, unique design that is *you*.

More than that, you've glimpsed how your personal "Island of One," once perhaps perceived as a place of solitary struggle, can radiate outward, becoming a beacon of strength, hope, and guidance for others. This final chapter, therefore, is not a destination or an ending. Oh no. It is a powerful commencement, a launching point. It's about the sacred art of weaving these seven fundamental principles, these potent keys to thriving, into the very warp and weft of your daily existence, transforming them from intellectual concepts into your lived, breathed, new normal. This is where you consciously choose to embark on a lifelong adventure, a continuous unfolding of purpose, meaning, and dynamic evolution. This is the space where you become, in the truest sense of the word, genuinely and authentically **unstoppable**.

Integrating the 7 Keys into the Fabric of Your Daily Life

The 7 Keys—Your Gifts, Your Time, Your Past, Your Plan, Your Needs, Your Fears, and Your Beliefs—are not dusty relics to be learned once during an intensive period of self-discovery and then respectfully filed away on a mental shelf. Absolutely not. They are vibrant, living principles, a dynamic toolkit to be actively, consciously, and skillfully used *every single day*, in the grand decisions and the seemingly mundane moments alike. True integration means these keys cease to be external concepts you "apply" and instead become an intrinsic part of your operational blueprint, as natural and essential to your way of being as the air you breathe. This is about cultivating an ongoing, moment-to-moment awareness and intentionality.

- **Daily Gift Activation:** Intentionally Deploying Your Strengths Every morning presents a fresh canvas. Begin each day by consciously asking, "How can I intentionally deploy my unique gifts today to navigate my tasks, enhance my interactions, and contribute meaningfully?" This isn't about grand gestures; it's about recognizing and utilizing your inherent strengths in everyday situations. Perhaps your gift for empathy can subtly transform a potentially difficult conversation at work into a moment of genuine understanding. Maybe your innate creativity can find an innovative, surprising solution to a nagging household problem. Or your hard-won resilience can help you face a minor setback—a frustrating traffic jam, a critical email—not with immediate frustration, but with a calm, quiet sense of "I can handle this. I've handled worse." Think of it as strategically choosing the right tool from your unique toolkit for the job at hand, every single time. For instance, if "patience" is a gift you've cultivated through challenging experiences, you might consciously activate it before a meeting you anticipate will be particularly challenging, allowing yourself to breathe and respond calmly.

- **Deliberate Time Investment: Honoring Your Most Precious Resource** Your time, my friend, is your life expressed in units. Continuously and honestly monitor how you are investing this irreplaceable currency. With each choice, ask: "Is this action, this commitment, this use of my next hour, truly aligned with my core priorities and my overarching 'Thrive Plan'?" Become a vigilant guardian against the "time robbers"—worry, want, and procrastination. These three are insidious thieves. For example, before mindlessly scrolling through social media, pause and genuinely ask if that's the highest and best use of that 30-minute window, or if investing it in a chapter of an inspiring book or a quick, heartfelt connection with a loved one would be more aligned with your thrive-ability. This isn't about rigid, joyless scheduling, but about conscious, value-driven allocation of your precious moments. I strive to "schedule every moment," even things like eating or going to the restroom (as I humorously recall from my Atari Laser Blast days where I was so engrossed, I didn't stop!). This might sound extreme, but for me, it's about maximizing efficiency and intentionality. I also "bunch like tasks together" to maintain focus, dedicating specific blocks of time for design work, writing, or meetings, rather than jumping frantically between disparate activities.

- **Past as Wisdom, Not Weight: Disarming Old Triggers** The echoes of your past will inevitably surface. Old patterns of thought, familiar anxieties, or knee-jerk reactions tied to past Significant Emotional Events (SEEs) may try to reassert themselves. When they do, greet them not with fear or frustration, but with the calm, discerning awareness of a seasoned observer. Recognize them for what they are: echoes, not current realities. Actively extract the embedded lesson, apply the distilled wisdom to your present situation, but steadfastly refuse to let those old emotional weights dictate your current actions or cloud your future vision. For instance, if a past business failure triggers a wave of paralyzing fear when you're considering a new venture, acknowledge the fear, yes. But then, recall the *specific, actionable* lessons learned from that failure (e.g., "I need a more robust financial plan this time," or "I need to delegate more effectively and trust my team"). Then, apply those lessons constructively to the new opportunity, rather than letting the generalized fear paralyze you. The past is your wise teacher, not your prison guard.

- **Living Your Plan: Daily Navigation with Your Roadmap**
  Your "Thrive Plan," with its S.M.A.R.T. goals, is not a static document to be created once and then forgotten in a drawer; it is your dynamic, daily roadmap for a purposeful life. Keep it accessible. Review its key components regularly—perhaps a quick glance at your weekly objectives each morning, or a more thorough review of monthly progress. Ask yourself, honestly: "Are my actions today, this week, actively moving me closer to my defined S.M.A.R.T. goals? If not, what course corrections are needed?" This consistent engagement keeps your plan alive and relevant, transforming it from a mere wish list into a practical, actionable guide for your daily decisions and efforts. If a goal is to improve physical health, your daily plan-living might involve scheduling those workouts, diligently planning healthy meals, and tracking your activity. It's about living *into* your plan, not just dreaming about it.

- **Honoring Your Needs: Fueling Your Inner Ecosystem**
  Become adept at checking in with your internal state. Truly listen to yourself. Are your core human needs—for safety and security, for love and belonging, for esteem and competence, for growth and self-actualization, for contribution—being adequately met? Make conscious choices throughout your day that nourish and honor these fundamental requirements. If you're feeling disconnected and lonely, proactively reach out to a friend or loved one

(honoring your need for belonging). If you're feeling stagnant or bored, dedicate time to learning something new, however small (honoring your need for growth). Recognizing and addressing these needs prevents the insidious buildup of frustration or burnout that can derail your journey. This could mean having the courage to say "no" to an extra commitment if your need for rest and rejuvenation (safety/physiological) is paramount. I've learned the hard way the importance of saying "no" to protect my time and energy, recognizing that my mental and emotional health is a top, non-negotiable priority.

- **Befriending Fear Moments: Courage as a Daily Practice**
  Fear, my friend, will inevitably arise as you stretch your boundaries and pursue truly meaningful goals. **I have nothing but truth an examples on this one.** When it does, do not shrink from it or allow it to dictate your actions. Acknowledge its presence calmly, almost like greeting an old, familiar—if unwelcome—acquaintance: "Ah, there's that feeling of fear again, showing up right on cue." Then, listen to it, not as a command, but as a messenger: "What is this fear *trying* to tell me? Is there a legitimate risk I need to mitigate, or is this just an old, familiar pattern trying to keep me small and safe?" Armed with this awareness, consciously *choose courage*. Take the next small, manageable step forward despite the fear. Each time you act in the face of fear, even a tiny act, you diminish its power and powerfully build your courage muscle. This could be as simple as making that phone call you've been dreading for days or sharing a new idea in a meeting when you fear judgment. The act itself, however small, is the victory.

- **Belief Reinforcement: Rewiring Your Internal Software**
  The profound work of reshaping your beliefs (that powerful Key #7) is an ongoing process of rewiring your internal software. Consciously and consistently practice your new, empowering beliefs. Repeat your affirmations with genuine feeling and conviction, letting them sink into your bones. Engage in vivid visualization, seeing yourself already living from this empowered belief system. Most importantly, act "as if" these beliefs are already your unshakeable truth, even when you don't quite feel it yet. When old, limiting thoughts or self-doubts resurface, actively challenge them. Remind yourself of the evidence that supports your new beliefs. This diligent, consistent reinforcement strengthens the neural pathways of your desired mindset, making it your new, powerful default. For example, if you're cultivating the belief "I am a capable and resourceful problem-solver," when a challenge arises, instead of defaulting to "Oh no, I can't handle this," consciously tell yourself, "I have the skills and creativity within me to figure this out," and then approach the problem from that empowered stance. Your thoughts create your reality.

This daily, moment-to-moment integration isn't about achieving an impossible standard of perfection. It's about consistent, conscious effort. It's about making these seven powerful principles the foundational, default operating system of your "Island of One," guiding your thoughts, feelings, and actions towards a life of authentic thriving. It's about choosing, again and again, to show up for yourself.

CHAPTER XV: Living a Life of Purpose and Meaning, Every Single Day

Strategies for Long-Term Growth and Preventing Backsliding

The journey of personal growth and transformation is not a linear ascent; it's a dynamic, often beautifully cyclical, process. There will be exhilarating moments of profound progress, insightful breakthroughs, and joyful expansion. And, inevitably, there will be times when old habits, familiar doubts, or external pressures try to pull you back into previous, less empowered states. It's okay. It's part of the human journey. Sustaining your "thrive-ability"— your capacity to not just reach but maintain and continually enhance your state of flourishing—requires ongoing vigilance, intentional strategies, and a deep, unwavering commitment to your own evolution.

- **The Unchanging Nature of Change** The only true constant in life is change. The world around you shifts, your circumstances evolve, and you, as an individual, are in a perpetual state of becoming. Therefore, a commitment to lifelong learning and adaptation is paramount. Embrace curiosity as a core value. Be perpetually open to new information, diverse perspectives, and innovative strategies. What worked effectively for you yesterday, or last year, might require thoughtful tweaking or even a complete overhaul to remain effective tomorrow. For instance, a career strategy that was successful a decade ago might be completely obsolete in today's rapidly changing job market. A communication style that served you well in one relationship might need adapting for a new one. The ability to learn, unlearn, and relearn is a hallmark of sustained thriving. This might mean deliberately reading books outside your usual genre, taking courses in unfamiliar subjects, or actively seeking feedback from people with different viewpoints than your own.

- **Your Personal Navigation System** Just as a ship's captain regularly checks their course and makes adjustments for wind and current, you must schedule periodic check-ins with yourself. These are not casual afterthoughts but deliberate, scheduled appointments for self-reflection and strategic alignment. Whether weekly, monthly, or quarterly, take dedicated time to:

    o   Review your "Thrive Plan": Are your overarching goals still relevant and inspiring? Do they still light you up?
    o   Assess your progress towards your S.M.A.R.T. goals: What's working well? Where are you encountering friction or resistance?
    o   Honestly evaluate your integration of the 7 Keys: Are you consistently activating your gifts, managing your time, processing your past constructively, honoring your needs, befriending your fears, and reinforcing empowering beliefs? Be brutally honest, but kind.
    o   Identify necessary adjustments: Do your goals need to be modified? Do your strategies require refinement? Are new priorities emerging that need your attention? This process of review and recalibration ensures that you remain on course, responsive to changing conditions, and deeply connected to what truly matters to you.

- **Celebrate Milestones, No Matter How Small** The human brain is hardwired to respond beautifully to positive reinforcement. Acknowledging and celebrating your progress, even the seemingly tiny steps forward, is absolutely crucial for fueling motivation and reinforcing positive behaviors. Don't defer your sense of accomplishment until you reach the grand, ultimate victory. Every disciplined choice, every fear overcome, every limiting belief challenged, every action taken in alignment with your plan—each of these is a milestone worthy of recognition. This celebration doesn't have to be extravagant; it can be a quiet moment of self-acknowledgment, sharing your progress with a supportive friend who *gets* it, or treating yourself to a small, meaningful reward. This creates a powerful positive feedback loop that makes the journey infinitely more enjoyable and sustainable.

- **Cultivating a Supportive Ecosystem** You are profoundly, undeniably influenced by your environment—the people you spend time with, the information you consume, the physical spaces you inhabit, and the experiences you engage in. To sustain your thrive-ability, consciously curate an environment that supports your growth and aligns with your highest values.

    o **People:** Seriously, surround yourself with individuals who genuinely uplift you, inspire you, challenge you constructively, and truly believe in your potential. These are your "thrive tribe." My conversations with Chip Yates, Bill Mitchell, Josh Roche, and Angelo Lombardo on "Life Can Change" are prime examples of this. Their diverse experiences and unwavering resilience constantly challenge and inspire me to be better, to keep pushing.

- Information: Be incredibly mindful of your media diet. Consume content that truly educates, inspires, and expands your perspective. Limit your exposure to excessive negativity, fear-mongering, or trivial distractions that mercilessly drain your mental and emotional energy. I strongly advocate for turning off the TV and minimizing distractions, because I've found that "noise" in our lives—worry, want, and procrastination—prevents us from focusing on what truly matters and from hearing our own inner voice.

- Experiences: Actively seek out experiences that stretch you, bring you profound joy, and connect you to your purpose and passions. Simultaneously, be willing to set healthy boundaries or even distance yourself from influences—whether people, situations, or information sources—that consistently drain your energy, trigger old negative patterns, or actively undermine your efforts to live an empowered life. Your environment is your garden; cultivate it carefully.

- **The Art of Bouncing Forward Gently** There will be times when you slip. It's inevitable. You'll fall back into an old habit, react from a place of fear, or fall short of an intention you set for yourself. This is *not* a sign of failure; it is an intrinsic, messy, beautiful, human part of the growth experience. In these moments, the most powerful response is not harsh self-criticism or endlessly berating yourself for imperfection. No. It is **self-compassion**. Treat yourself with the same kindness, understanding, and encouragement you would offer a dear friend who was struggling. Acknowledge the setback without judgment: "Okay, I didn't handle that situation as skillfully as I'd hoped." Learn from it: "What can I understand from this, and what will I do differently next time?" And then, gently and firmly, guide yourself back on course. Every "failure" creates a new Significant Emotional Event in your life. *You decide how it will impact your life.* Choose to make the impact one of learning and renewed commitment, fueled by self-compassion, not self-condemnation.

Sustaining your thrive-ability is an active, engaged process. It's about building not just a resilient foundation, but also the ongoing practices and mindsets that allow you to continue growing, adapting, and flourishing throughout the ever-changing landscape of your life. It's a marathon, not a sprint, and every step counts.

Embracing Lifelong Learning and Adaptation as Your Greatest Adventure

The alluring concept of finally "arriving" at a static destination—of being perfectly "fixed," completely "healed," or permanently "perfected"—is, in truth, an illusion, a beautiful mirage that can actually distract from the real, profound beauty of the path itself. Life, in its most vibrant and meaningful expression, is not a problem to be solved or a state to be achieved and then maintained indefinitely. No. It is a continuous, dynamic journey of evolution, an unending process of becoming. The moment you believe you have all the answers, the moment you feel you've "made it" and there's nothing more to learn or discover, is often the precise moment you cease to truly grow and begin to stagnate. It's like a video game where you've collected all the power-ups and then just stand there, wondering what's next, missing the whole point of the game.

Therefore, the unstoppable you embraces lifelong learning and adaptation not as a burdensome chore, but as one of life's greatest and most exhilarating adventures. Cultivate an insatiable curiosity about yourself, about others, about the world around you. Actively seek out new challenges that stretch your current capacities, push your comfort zones, and invite you to develop new skills and perspectives. Be courageous enough to unlearn outdated beliefs or behaviors that no longer serve your highest good, even if they once felt comfortable or essential.

The principles and tools offered in this book provide a powerful and adaptable toolkit, a compass and a set of navigating instruments, but your unique application of them will, and *should*, evolve as you yourself evolve and as your life circumstances shift. The profound joy and deepest meaning are often found not in reaching some mythical endpoint, but in the rich, vibrant tapestry of the journey itself—in the continuous learning, the surprising discoveries, the thrilling moments of connection, the challenges bravely overcome, and the constant, exciting unfolding of who you are becoming. This is not about a restless dissatisfaction, but a joyful, engaged participation in the dynamic dance of life.

And remember that potent quote, that crucial, non-negotiable mantra for the truly unstoppable you: "Remove the word 'Later' from your vocabulary as it is the worst killer of a dream." This isn't just about time; "later" is far more than just a temporal marker. It is often the silk-lined coffin where dreams, aspirations, and vital life changes are laid to rest, prematurely and unnecessarily.

"Later" whispers seductive promises of a "perfect moment" that rarely, if ever, truly arrives—a future state where you'll feel "more ready," "less busy," or "better equipped." This, my friend, is a dangerous illusion. It's the ultimate procrastinator's paradise, where nothing ever gets done.

If there is a change you *know* in your heart you need to make, a skill you yearn to develop, a relationship you need to mend or cultivate, a creative project that calls to your soul, or a dream that sets your spirit alight, the most potent and empowered time to act is invariably **now**. Not when all the stars align perfectly. Not when all your fears have magically vanished. Not when you feel an absolute guarantee of success. **Now.** Take the first step, however small, however imperfect, however tentative it may feel. That initial action, like the first turn of a massive flywheel, is often the hardest, but it is the one that breaks the inertia. It is the spark that ignites the flame. Action, even imperfect action, creates clarity, builds momentum, and opens doors that remain firmly shut to passive contemplation. As Zig Ziglar wisely reminds us, "You can not change your destination overnight but you can change the direction right now." The power to alter your trajectory, to begin building the life you truly desire, resides in the immediate choices and actions of this present moment.

Final Call to Action: "Are you ready to make it count?"

You now stand at a powerful threshold, equipped with a comprehensive blueprint for your "Island of One." You possess a deeper understanding of your inherent gifts, the undeniable power of your choices, and the seven transformative keys designed to unlock a life of profound and unstoppable resilience, authentic purpose, and deep, abiding meaning. The truth remains steadfast: you are, and always have been, intrinsically built to thrive. The remarkable journey to fully realizing and expressing this magnificent, innate design is not a one-time event but an ongoing, unfolding tapestry woven with daily opportunities for growth, for genuine connection, for meaningful contribution, and for continuous evolution.

The question, therefore, is not a one-time query but a daily affirmation, a moment-to-moment internal check-in that only *you* can answer: **Are you truly ready to make this day, this choice, this interaction, this challenge, count?**

Are you ready, today and every day, to step fully and courageously into your inherent power, to embrace the unique landscape of your island not as a confining limitation but as your personal, powerful launchpad into a life of your own deliberate design? Are you ready to live with clear intention, to allow your authentic light to shine brightly and without apology, and to meticulously, joyfully build a life that resonates not with societal expectations or past limitations, but with the deepest wellsprings of your unique potential and makes a genuine, positive difference in the world, however *you* define that?

The choice, as it has always been and will always be, rests entirely and unequivocally with you. Your thriving life is not a distant mirage; it is a present possibility, awaiting your conscious and courageous engagement. Go forth and live deliberately. Embrace your power. Shine your light. The adventure is yours, and it is happening now. Your thriving life awaits, not in some far-off future, but in the choices you make today, and every day that follows. You are unstoppable.

Island of One: Born Different. Build to Thrive

CHAPTER XVI

Lead your Life: Speaking, Coaching, and Mentorship

"Your thriving life is not a distant hope; it is an imminent reality, a potentiality humming with energy, waiting for your conscious, courageous, and continuous 'Yes!"

The journey we've taken through these pages is designed to be a catalyst—a spark that ignites your own resilience and reframes what's possible. The COMPASS system is a powerful blueprint for designing a life that is not just survived, but truly thrived.

But a blueprint is just the beginning. Sometimes, to build a truly unshakeable life, you need an architect to walk the site with you. To truly shift a team's mindset, you need a guide to lead the conversation.

This book is your map. The following are ways I can help you and your team navigate the territory. If you are ready to take the principles of *Island of One* from the page and bring them to life for your organization, here are the ways we can work together.

Bring the COMPASS System to Your Stage: Keynote Speaking

There is a unique energy that comes from a shared, live experience. As a keynote speaker, my goal is not just to motivate, but to equip your audience with a new framework for thinking about their inner world. My presentations are not lectures; they are immersive, story-driven experiences designed to be raw, authentic, and immediately applicable.

Popular Topics Include:

- **Born Different, Built to Thrive:** Turning Your Unique Challenges into Your Greatest Strengths
- **The COMPASS System:** A Leader's Blueprint for Designing a Life of Purpose
- **From External Validation to Internal Knowing:** The Secret to Unshakeable Confidence
- **Your Island as a Beacon:** How Your Story Can Inspire and Lead Others

Your team will leave not just inspired, but armed with the practical tools and the mental reframes needed to face their next challenge with confidence and clarity.

To inquire about booking me for your next conference, summit, or corporate event, please visit www.jasonmcclain.com/speaking.

In the Foxhole with You: Strategic Advising & Coaching

Sometimes you don't need a speech; you need a strategist in the trenches with you. For a select number of clients, I offer private advising and coaching engagements designed to guide leaders and their teams through the entire COMPASS process.

For Leadership Teams: We work together to conduct a full "Values Audit," identify the core strategic pivots for personal and professional growth, and build a 90-day battle plan to execute the relaunch. This is an intensive engagement designed to create alignment, clarity, and immediate momentum when the stakes are highest.

For the Entrepreneur: This is a one-on-one coaching relationship for the founder or CEO at a crossroads. We go deep on the personal and professional challenges of designing a purposeful life, focusing on building the inner resilience required to lead with confidence and make the tough decisions.

These engagements are for those who are ready to do the hard work and are committed to creating real, lasting change.

To explore a private advising or coaching engagement, please visit www.jasonmcclain.com/coaching to submit an application.

The Immersion: Interactive Workshops & Events

The quickest way to master a new skill is to practice it. Throughout the year, we host exclusive workshops and immersive events designed to be hands-on training camps for individuals who are ready to become the captain of their own lives. These are not passive seminars. You will work alongside a curated group of your peers to:

- Run your personal and professional challenges through the COMPASS Decision Matrix.
- Develop and pressure-test your 90-Day Battle Plan for personal growth.
- Build and cultivate your Thrive Tribe in a real-world setting.

These events are the ultimate opportunity to move from theory to practice and to forge powerful relationships with other leaders who are committed to bouncing forward.

CHAPTER XVI: Lead Your Life: Speaking, Coaching, and Mentorship

To see a schedule of upcoming events and learn more, please visit www.jasonmcclain.com/events.

CONCLUSION

Your Thriving Life Awaits

"Your thriving life is not a distant hope; it is an imminent reality, a potentiality humming with energy, waiting for your conscious, courageous, and continuous 'Yes!"

We've journeyed together through the unique landscape of your "Island of One," uncovering the seven essential keys that unlock the door to a life of profound resilience and authentic fulfillment. From unearthing your innate **Gifts** to mastering your **Time**, from reclaiming your **Past** to charting your deliberate **Plan**, from honoring your Core **Needs** to bravely befriending your **Fears** and, ultimately, to reshaping the very **Beliefs** that form the operating system of your island—you now hold a blueprint. Not just any blueprint, but *your* blueprint, meticulously designed to navigate your unique terrain and to prove, unequivocally, that you are indeed built to thrive.

The core message, the truth that has echoed through these pages and, I truly hope, now resonates deeply within your spirit, is this: **You are already magnificent.** The capacity to create a life

CHAPTER XVI: Lead Your Life: Speaking, Coaching, and Mentorship

brimming with purpose, joy, and meaning is not a distant prize to be won, nor a quality reserved for a chosen few. It is your birthright, an inherent part of your magnificent design. Remember, **"God already gave what you need to do what He wants you to do."** The tools, the strength, the resilience—they are not additions you must desperately seek, like something missing. No, they are powerful endowments you already possess, waiting to be fully uncovered, embraced, and activated by you.

Think back to that painful "one-handed-monkey" taunt, a moment that could have easily defined me by limitation, by a deficit. Instead, it became a catalyst, a testament to the powerful truth that our perceived disadvantages, our unique "islands," are often the very crucibles that forge our greatest strengths. Your island, with all its specific challenges and distinct contours, is not a testament to deficit, but a powerful declaration of your unique capacity to adapt, to innovate, and to overcome. It has shaped you, prepared you, and equipped you in ways you might only now be starting to fully appreciate. It's your training ground.

The journey you've undertaken through this book has been about stripping away the illusions—the illusion of your fear as an insurmountable barrier, the illusion of your past as an unchangeable destiny, the illusion that you are somehow lacking or incomplete. It has been about replacing those illusions with empowering truths: that your fear can be a powerful messenger, your past a collection of invaluable data, and your unique design the very source of your unstoppable power.

As you step forward from these pages, carry with you the unwavering conviction that you are the captain of your choices and the architect of your reality. The power to transform your life, to build bridges from where you are to where you dream of being, rests firmly and squarely with *you*. The seven keys are now securely in your hand. The principles of resilience are etched into your understanding. You've learned to silence the external noise and that nagging internal critic, to listen instead to the deep wisdom of your own heart, and to honor the fundamental needs of your being.

This, my friend, is not an ending, but a vibrant commencement. The world awaits the unique light that only *you* can shine. It awaits the contribution that only *you*, with your specific gifts and experiences, can make. The **"Island of One"** is no longer a place of isolation, but your sovereign territory, your launchpad, your beacon. From this powerful place of strength and self-knowing, your capacity to connect authentically, to love deeply, and to contribute meaningfully is amplified beyond measure.

So, the question remains, the one that echoes from the very beginning, the one that I hope you'll ask yourself every single day: **Are you ready to make it count?**

Are you ready, today and every day, to take this blueprint, this profound understanding, this newfound awareness of your own magnificent design, and build a life that doesn't just exist, but truly thrives? A life that resonates with your deepest values, your most cherished dreams, and your most authentic self, without apology?

Your thriving life is not a distant hope; it is an imminent reality, a potentiality humming with energy, waiting for your conscious, courageous, and continuous **"Yes!"** Go forth and live deliberately. Embrace your power. Shine your light. The adventure is yours, and it is happening now. Your thriving life awaits, not in some far-off future, but in the choices you make today, and every day that follows. You are unstoppable.

Island of One: Born Different. Build to Thrive

JOIN THE ISLAND

Congratulations! You've completed a significant step in your journey with "Island of One," demonstrating your dedication to personal growth and self-discovery. Now that you intimately understand the power of the **C.O.M.P.A.S.S. System's** methodology, including the precise scoring process and critical checks and balances, your next step is to access the interactive digital tool that brings it all to life. Ready to build an unstoppable, purposeful life with confidence and clarity? Your adventure continues at **IslandofOne.com!**

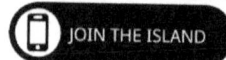

Ready to build an unstoppable, purposeful life? Your adventure continues at IslandofOne.com!

This isn't just a website; it's your dedicated online sanctuary and a thriving community designed to empower you to deepen your understanding and seamlessly apply the principles of "Island of One."

At Islandof0ne.com, you'll unlock a wealth of resources, including:

- **Exclusive Video Training Program:** Dive deeper into core concepts with our comprehensive "Island of One" video series, designed to take your learning to the next level.
- **Downloadable Workbook:** Put principles into practice immediately with our complete workbook, a perfect companion to the video program.
- **Free Webinars & New Programs:** Gain fresh insights and stay ahead with complimentary webinars and access to our latest transformative content.
- **Supportive Membership Community:** Join a vibrant network of like-minded individuals committed to living deliberately. Share experiences, gain support, and accelerate your growth.
- **Immersive Conferences & Events:** Connect in person at upcoming events, designed for powerful learning and fostering connections that truly matter.

This entire program is your essential next step after finishing the book. We are here to help you not just survive, but truly flourish and become stronger and better.

Don't wait! Visit Islandof0ne.com today and take the courageous next step towards your unstoppable life by registering on our website!

Island of One: Born Different. Build to Thrive

Island of One: Born Different. Build to Thrive

LISTEN TO THE

CRUSH & CLIMB PODCAST

Hosted by Jason McClain

Pour yourself a glass of something you love and join us for *Crush & Climb*, (www.crushandclimb.com) the podcast that pairs the intricate stories of great wine with the powerful strategies needed to navigate life's biggest challenges. This isn't just another business podcast. It's a weekly ritual for leaders, entrepreneurs, and anyone with the courage to turn adversity into their greatest advantage. Hosted by author, speaker, and winery owner Jason McClain, *Crush & Climb* is your guide to building a life and business that are not just successful, but significant. Each episode begins with "The Pour," where Jason uncorks a bottle of wine whose character,

history, and flavor profile mirror the day's core lesson. From a bold Cabernet Sauvignon that speaks of legacy to a crisp Sauvignon Blanc that embodies the art of saying "no," the wine is more than a drink—it's a metaphor, a conversation starter, and a reminder to savor the journey. From there, we dive into "The Forge"—the heart of the episode where raw experience is hammered into practical wisdom. Drawing from his own dramatic journey of failures and triumphs, Jason shares unfiltered stories and actionable frameworks designed to help you not just bounce back from setbacks, but to bounce forward with newfound strength and clarity.

Our Guiding Philosophies: Two Sides of the Same Coin

The *Crush & Climb* podcast is built on two foundational pillars, drawn from Jason McClain's books, that address the interconnected challenges of business and life:

1. **Island of One: Navigating Your Inner World**

   External success is meaningless without internal strength. The "Island of One" philosophy speaks to the personal journey. It's for anyone who has ever felt different, isolated, or underestimated. It's about transforming perceived limitations into your most formidable superpowers. Here, we unpack the COMPASS System, a guide to designing a life of purpose and fulfillment by mastering your inner world:
   - **C - Clarity:** Defining your plan with S.M.A.R.T. goals.
   - **O - Ownership:** Taking radical responsibility for your choices.
   - **M - Manage:** Mastering your time and energy.
   - **P - Perspective:** Understanding that your past is data, not destiny.

- **A - Acknowledge:** Befriending your fears to feed your faith.
- **S - Satisfy:** Meeting your own needs without guilt.
- **S - Surround:** Building your "Thrive Tribe" for support and growth.

2. **Pivot to Profit: Mastering the Business Turnaround**

   Life and business rarely move in a straight line. The "Pivot to Profit" philosophy is for the leader staring down a crisis, the entrepreneur whose great idea has stalled, or the sales team that has lost its momentum. It's about facing brutal facts, finding the hidden opportunities within a crisis, and executing a disciplined plan to capture them. Through this lens, we explore the R.I.S.E. System, a four-part framework for engineering a powerful comeback:
   - **R - Reckon:** Conducting a "business autopsy" to find the root cause of a problem without blame.
   - **I - Identify:** Pinpointing the "painkiller" solution your market desperately needs.
   - **S - Strategize:** Building a 90-day battle plan to turn opportunity into revenue.
   - **E - Execute:** Cultivating the resilience to withstand setbacks and bounce forward.

Who Is This Podcast For?

Crush & Climb is for you if:

- You are an entrepreneur or business owner facing uncertainty and looking for a proven roadmap to stabilize and scale.
- You are a leader or executive responsible for guiding a team through challenging times and want to foster a culture of resilience and psychological safety.

- You are at a personal or professional crossroads, feeling stuck and seeking the clarity and courage to design your next chapter.
- You believe that success is holistic—that professional achievement and personal fulfillment are deeply intertwined.
- You appreciate the finer things in life, like a great glass of wine, and believe that life's lessons can be found in the most unexpected places.

Join the *Crush & Climb* community. Subscribe today wherever you get your podcasts, and let's raise a glass to the journey ahead. It's time to crush your challenges, climb to new heights, and build a legacy you can be proud of.

Island of One: Born Different. Build to Thrive

ABOUT THE AUTHOR

JASON MCCLAIN is a distinguished entrepreneur, celebrated author, and impactful keynote speaker, boasting over three decades of experience empowering individuals to unlock their full potential. His impressive entrepreneurial journey includes founding and successfully divesting over a dozen companies across various sectors, cementing his expertise in the digital landscape for two decades.

His life, marked by unparalleled resilience stemming from a unique personal challenge, cultivated exceptional adaptability and innovative problem-solving, teaching him to view every obstacle as a catalyst for profound growth.

As a highly sought-after speaker, Jason delivers inspiring messages to diverse audiences, from intimate small groups to thousands at major conferences and events. He has spoken for organizations like Disney, CBS, and ABC, and led team-building programs for Pepsi and other Fortune 50 companies. He shares practical strategies for fostering a `"growth mindset," making critical decisions, and transforming adversity into triumph.

Beyond business, Jason is a motivator known for helping people find passion in life, authoring books that focus on turning challenges into solutions. He also owns a luxury wine brand, McClain Cellars, with multiple locations and makes wine for other brands, businesses, restaurants and offers award-winning wines the public.

His integrity and business acumen are widely recognized, earning him an Honorary Doctorate of Divinity. Married for over 20 years, he and his wife joyfully raise their three daughters, attributing much of his success to his family's unwavering support.

Jason continues to innovate, helping people build businesses and design lives on their own terms.

To learn more about working with Jason or his team visit **www.jasonmcclain.com** or reach out to him on social media at @jasoncmcclain.

Watch Jason's videos, attend his private events, or read his other books...

PIVOT TO PROFIT:
Turning Failures into Fuel

New Book Available Today

Visit JasonMcClain.com to learn more about his programs and become a part of the message.

Island of One: Born Different. Build to Thrive

Ready to build an unstoppable, purposeful life? Your adventure continues at Islandofone.com!

Follow Jason on Social Media!
@jasoncmcclain

www.breakthroughpublishing.net

Island of One

Born Different. Built to Thrive.

www.ingramcontent.com/pod-product-compliance
Lightning Source LLC
Chambersburg PA
CBHW070754230426
43665CB00017B/2360